The
ART *of*
ILLUSION

The ART of ILLUSION

A Trompe l'Oeil
PAINTING COURSE

JANET SHEARER

NORTH LIGHT BOOKS
Cincinnati, Ohio

Contents

Introduction 6

Design and Perspective 12

Preparation and Equipment 32

Painting a Mural 48

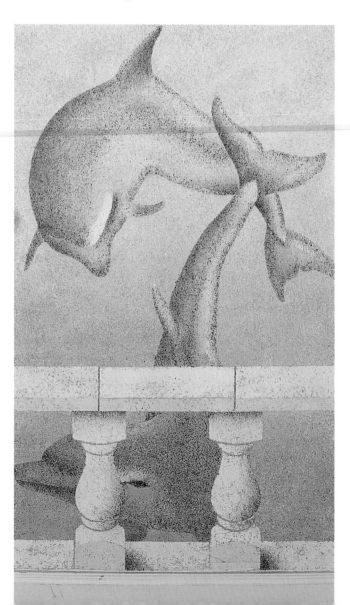

The Projects

Tuscan View 62

Tabby Cat 70

Guinea Fowl 74

Cattle Murals 78

En Grisaille 82

Changing Room 88

The Monk 94

A Cornish Window 98

The White Horses 104

Painted Furniture 114

Tiepolo Mural 118

The Arches 120

Working to Commission 138

Addresses 140

Acknowledgments 141

Index 142

Introduction

We can trace the history of murals right back to the time when cavemen drew and painted on the rough walls of their dwellings. They described the animals and nature which surrounded them with tremendous anatomical accuracy. The inhabitants of those caves simply scratched on to the rock, rubbing color made from ground minerals into the scored marks. These images, sometimes drawn only with charcoal, still delight us ten thousand years later.

There isn't room in this book to do justice to a history of this type of painting. It's a fascinating subject in itself because we have recorded lifestyles, cultures, wars and rituals, not to mention extraordinary religious events. We are fortunate that these paintings have been preserved all over the world, in tombs, religious buildings and even those earliest of all homes.

Although the Greeks may have invented trompe l'oeil, it was the Romans who developed it from ordinary decorative painting in order to increase the feeling of space in a room. By using theatrical architecture they created extraordinary illusions to adorn bare walls.

Translated from French, trompe l'oeil means 'trick the eye', and although it really is just a visual joke, the joke is only effective if you do it well. And that is what this book will teach you.

The wonderful thing about trompe l'oeil is its ability to change our surroundings and bring a little fantasy into our lives. On a grey winter's day, a painting like this can add warmth and color to a room, leading your eye out through the wall to far-off places (in this case, Tuscany!).

Trompe l'oeil distinguishes itself from ordinary decorative murals by its intent to deceive, and it is this which sets it apart from ordinary still-life painting. The artist's technical skill is meant to go undetected and, with the use of perfect perspective, cleverly observed light and realistic colors, the trick is to make the onlooker believe that a flat surface is not flat, or that a space exists where there is no space. A trompe l'oeil painting is one which shows apparently three-dimensional objects and spaces in a way which the eye accepts as realism in the context of their surroundings.

So why paint a trompe l'oeil?

The answer is simply for fun! Human beings love to use their power of observation to record lifestyles, longings, cultures and social trends. We have an innate sense of decoration and will always want to use whatever materials we can to enhance our surroundings. What is especially interesting is that we use trompe l'oeil and murals as a statement of permanence – a mark of identity, part of the architecture – and I hope to encourage you to try this in your own home.

Cheering up a rather plain pine fireplace can be fun if you've got time and patience! This one was first painted to look like marble, then I 'inset' some 'mosaic' panels which were copied from an amazing fireplace seen in a very grand house.

We love color, texture, humor and illusion. Painting a mural means using them all. We like to change walls from the bland, bare anonymity of a single color to tell a story. Once a mural exists on a wall, that plain surface is lost, changed into another world in another dimension.

Nowadays too many of us have lost confidence in our own creative abilities because we don't believe we can match the expertise of professional artists. Whilst I don't deny the magic and mystique that some folk are fortunate enough to be born with, the skill to draw and paint well can be learnt and, given a little practical guidance, anyone can do it!

My motivation for writing this book has been witnessing at first hand, during my short time of teaching, the pleasure people experience when they realize they can achieve the painting they have pictured in their mind because they have been shown how to. Unleashed into a fantasy world of make-believe, released from the confines of diminutive works of art, and maybe at the same time escaping from humdrum buildings, you can, with a bit of sensible help and advice, develop your own ideas into the most wonderful illusions.

How to learn

During the three years that I have been inviting people to join me for a five-day introduction to mural painting, I have seen spectacular results. People have come from all over the world hungry for knowledge. I now know with absolute certainty that if you have the skill to write your name, then by cultivating your powers of observation you can learn to draw and then to paint.

I put together the course upon which this book is based, firstly sourcing an idea, developing it into a workable design drawn to scale, introducing the use of perspective, preparation of surfaces, assembling materials, and finally the magical experience of putting the design on to the wall using the confidence gained by understanding how to do it and marvelling at the unlimited versatility of the paint!

My objective has always been to furnish visitors to my studio with the skill to attempt a mural of their own, whilst making it clear that to become a master of this art takes much longer than five days and requires dedication, perseverance and a great deal of patience.

Anyone can do it!

I never intended to paint murals. I loved to paint 'big' and came from a very creative family where this sort of behaviour was acceptable. After art college, where I studied fine art and lost confidence as a painter, I became a photographic model in the fashion and advertising industry, which led me into the world of film and television and introduced me to set-building. It was fast, efficient and exciting and it taught me that only the essentials are important when producing an effect.

Seduced by the excitement of film-making, I became, in quick succession, a stylist responsible for choosing props, then a set-dresser, then a bona fide member of the Associated Cinematographic and Television Technicians and worked my way up to Art Director. This was when the big change came about.

I had designed the set for a television commercial for a bank, employing a scenic artist to paint a bird 10 metres (11 yards) in diameter, typical of the bank's logo, on the studio floor. To my horror, I noticed after his departure that the bird's wings were wrong! I decided to repaint it myself overnight. When the film crew arrived in the morning, no-one knew what had happened. My delicate reputation as a junior art director was safe, as was the reputation of the scenic artist. What had also happened, though, was a revelation to me. I had had more fun doing the painting than watching someone else do it!

Over the next few years I became a scenic artist with the help and guidance of Ken Hill, a master of the art, and his wife Nina, also an amazing painter. I learnt how to paint enormous cloths with less effort than you would imagine, how to be economical with painted statements by understating something and making suggestions of forms rather than describing them in detail. I mastered the mixing of color and how to use color effectively to give the impression of realism. I learnt about eye-levels in relation to the camera height. I tackled perspective, light sources, how to paint trees and grass, sky, clouds, buildings – you name it, Ken had a special method of dealing with it.

My first trompe l'oeil

The turning point for me came when someone connected with the film industry asked me to paint a mural around an indoor swimming pool in London's Hyde Park Square. The glass roof was two floors above the pool and all the walls were to be included in the design. Although I had a young baby at the time, I accepted the commission, taking on an assistant who painted and helped with the baby when required. Sophie and I painted that trompe l'oeil under the most impossible conditions. However, the finished work was extensively photographed and was responsible for my launch into the world of mural painting.

After that, mural commissions came thick and fast. I have painted walls and ceilings in restaurants, pubs, hotels and private houses in the UK and abroad. Some of the larger commissions included a trompe l'oeil at Heathrow airport's Terminal Three, two at Mormon temples, a huge single panel for the town of Tavistock in Devon, and the whole wall of the main bar on board the *Oriana*, one of the world's largest cruise liners. Each project brought its own upheavals, problems and challenges. The final results have always brought both relief and satisfaction for myself and, I hope, for my clients. And the thrill of looking at the blank space on the wall before I start has never left me.

Painting a mural in order to satisfy your own natural sense of decoration is an achievable goal, and great happiness can be found in the pursuit of achievable goals! Do try it!

Janet Shearer

This was my first trompe l'oeil. At the time it seemed quite small compared with some of the film scenery I had been painting, but actually it was two floors high! The original glass roof was later replaced which unfortunately cut through the top of my painted arch, as you can see here.

Design and Perspective

Designing your own trompe l'oeil is as important as painting it. Something has motivated you to make this huge statement. What is it? For some reason the blank surface of the wall at which you gaze impedes your view of what is beyond, and at this first stage, the world is your oyster!

Perhaps your room has started to feel claustrophobic and you long to burst through into a panoramic landscape you once knew in Tuscany. Perhaps you yearn for a classical grandeur that you could never afford in your tiny basement apartment. Perhaps you have seen a beautifully painted trompe l'oeil in a restaurant and would like to have one yourself, or maybe you just want to make a small visual joke – putting your own stamp on the place you call home. It's your sign of permanence. It's your sign that you intend to stay there.

All murals have a reason for their existence. In this case, I wanted to keep a little bit of summer in our house right by the kitchen sink where it was most needed. Even in the middle of winter it makes us all feel warmer and brighter, and the flowers seem almost as fresh as real ones. This project is shown in more detail on page 98.

Gathering Ideas

How on earth do you start? Take a long, hard look at the room in question. Look at the furniture, at the existing architectural features and at the main light source. Think very carefully about your main viewpoint (by this I mean the place from which you most often will be seeing the painting). When you start to put your ideas down on paper, you need to consider where you are standing in the room.

Try to visualize your inspiration in the context of the room. You may at this stage only have a 'loose concept', but that's okay. Few of the great artists would know what to do without further hesitation. They would do exactly what you are going to do – retire to a comfy armchair with a huge pile of magazines and books featuring plenty of photographs of interiors and landscapes. Start to browse, keeping your original idea vaguely in your mind. Soon you will notice that you spot things relating to your own idea – the open window, that emotive Tuscan hillside, the French shutters you remember from your last holiday. All these should be marked, either with efficient sticky pieces of paper or with torn strips of newspaper. Gradually you will find your original idea blossoming, becoming more elaborate. You may even find that your early thoughts change and you discover something much more exciting. Keep your mind 'open'. I have often completely changed tack, and my first thoughts have been swept away after a couple of hours of serious browsing. This is called 'sourcing' and may extend to books on architecture, African wildlife, gardening, history and so on. A visit to the local library may well be required. All the time, keep your intended wall space fixed firmly in your mind.

When you find something that interests you, you may like to make a drawing or tracing of it as well as marking the page in the book. It is very unlikely that you will find what

Gathering ideas for a mural is like making a collage of things which interest you and which you can somehow include in your project. Magazines are an excellent source of material, especially if you don't mind tearing them up. Keep everything you find in a folder with all your doodles and sketches.

you want in just one photograph. You may have that wonderful snapshot taken at dawn on your honeymoon in the Swiss Alps, but you need a foreground window to frame the beautiful view, and that may be found in a magazine photo. You may end up with a lot of tracings of different sizes, but don't be alarmed! There is a simple method for enlarging and reducing drawings which requires little more than the ability to work out simple proportions (see page 57). Layout or tracing paper is cheap, and at this stage you can afford to do as many sketches as you like – a lot less costly than making enormous mistakes on the wall.

What you are looking for is an idea that works in the space you have available. If you are considering enlarging the room visually by leading the onlooker out through an apparent opening in the real wall, you must consider that the wall itself is the picture plane and the opening starts on this plane. Everything that is painted on this surface, as it were 'in the real world', will be life size, but as the eye is led through the opening into the imagined space, the composition is affected by perspective.

Don't expect to get it right first time. If you have trouble drawing something and are getting proportions wrong, turn it upside down to copy it. When an image is upside down, visual clues don't mean the same as when they are the right way up. Take your time and look at the picture. Your brain won't recognize it, but if you slowly work your way through the drawing, from top to bottom, looking at the angles and lines, and the way they join up like a jigsaw, you will be amazed to find that it is easier to copy something this way.

Lighting murals

Lighting has to be considered right at the outset of a project and provision made for electricity cables to be laid where required (this may mean channelling in the wall to be painted). A uniform lighting system works best with trompe l'oeil, because when you try to enhance the light artificially it can spoil your effect. It's also fatal to mix real architectural features with painted ones as the real ones cause lighting problems and unwanted shadows.

Use every means at your disposal to expand your idea. Obviously a camera is a marvellous tool, and if you can't find what you are looking for in someone else's photos, try to set up what you want yourself, and use the best equipment that you can to photograph your subject. When you photograph something, consider at the outset your eye-level (see page 18) and your light source (see page 31). This means that it helps to take the photograph of your subject from exactly the same height in relation to the subject as your viewpoint in the painting will be, rather than trying to adapt the drawing later.

If video cameras and computers appeal to you, use them. There are no limitations or rules to the process of designing a mural. It's relatively easy to 'freeze' a frame on a video if you've got the right equipment.

By now you will have a pile of ideas strewn around you. Well-known and successful artists can take weeks to make up their minds about something, so remember it is no good rushing into a weak design.

Turning Ideas into a Painting

Even if the subject you have chosen to paint doesn't appear to have any perspective, believe me, it has, and you will find this chapter of the book useful. Perspective is not something you add at the last minute. In fact, it's impossible to draw anything at all without understanding it. It is not something to be frightened of.

The information in this chapter applies to people working at different levels. You may find that for your first project you don't need to know about projections from plans and elevations, but knowing something about viewpoints, eye-levels and vanishing points does help.

I have shown here some perspective problems which were particularly relevant to the design of the mural of the Tuscan View. This trompe l'oeil painting was created as part of a kitchen wall, the idea being to show doors open on to a sunny patio, overlooking a hillside in Italy with distant mountains shimmering in the heat (see finished painting on facing page and on page 62).

Discovering perspective for yourself

In order to have a better understanding of perspective and be able to turn your sketched ideas into convincing illusions, all the following pages are relevant, but it will be useful for you to try one or two simple visual tests for yourself in order to understand the drawings shown here.

The first thing to establish when painting a mural is the place in the room from which you will most often look at the painting, in other words the main viewpoint (see also page 17). This is always important, but particularly in the design of something like this Tuscan View, when the width of 'view' visible, and the perspective of the foreground architecture need to be considered. In general, one stands centrally to look at a painting. When you look at a view through an opening, you see more of it standing close to the opening than you do if you take a few steps back (try doing this with a door or a window). Sometimes we have to pretend we are standing further away than we actually are able to in the room in order to minimize distortion which you will begin to understand as you read on.

Having chosen the viewpoint, the next thing to consider is the eye-level – your eye-level (see page 18). For all paintings this is something you need to master, and a few simple experiments can help you to understand how things work. A good way to understand the eye-level is to hold a pencil horizontally at arm's length in front of you at your eye-level and practise noticing where it is in relation to objects you are looking at, or a landscape or the interior of a room.

The position of the eye-level determines the shape of all the elements in your painting. It can best be thought of as an imaginary line encircling you at the level of your eyes. If something you are looking at is below your eye-level, its shape will be affected accordingly. If you look up to your subject you will be seeing it differently. In your mural, in order to achieve realism, you must think about where you are in relation to your subject.

Continues on page 22

Establishing the Main Viewpoint

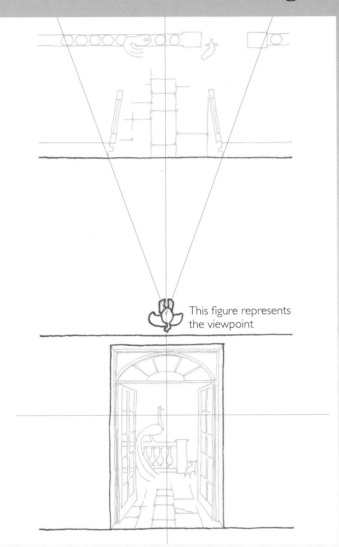

This figure represents the viewpoint

The first thing to establish is the main viewpoint by considering the most important place to look at the mural. When you look at a 'view' through an opening, you see more of it if you stand close to the opening than if you take a few steps back. It helps to imagine a bird's-eye view of the wall, your viewpoint in the real world and a plan of the imaginary elements as shown in the top drawing. Underneath is the view as you want to see it on the wall, based on sketches which have been done freehand, but you now need to formalize the drawing. On the right is the finished painting showing how important these first thoughts are.

Key
Black lines: *elements in real life, including edges of painted 'opening'*
Red lines: *eye-level*
Blue lines: *imaginary elements*
Green lines: *important 'construction' lines*

Positioning the Eye-level

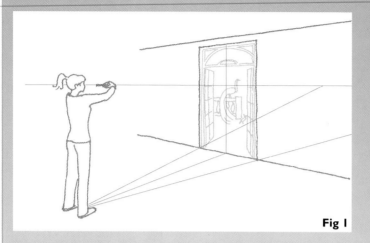

Fig 1

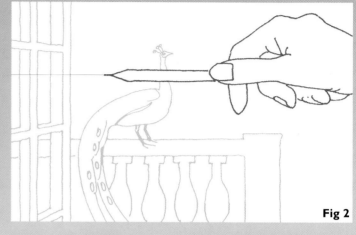

Fig 2

The eye-level is the imaginary line in front of your eyes which can be best understood by holding a pencil horizontally at arm's length in front of you and practising noticing where it is in relation to a landscape you are looking at, or the interior of a room (Fig 1). Also try seeing what happens to the shape of objects around you in relation to the pencil held in front of you when you sit down or stand on a chair. (i.e. what happens to the lines which form the edges of objects when compared with the horizontal line formed by the pencil).

For all my designs, I use a measurement of 1.5 m (5 ft) from the ground line (i.e. my feet) to my eye-level as a standard height and this level is always shown in red on the diagram. In the drawing above (Fig 2), having worked out my viewpoint I now need to establish the eye-level for the project. Try to imagine whether you would look up to your subject or whether it is lower than your own eye-level, like the little dog shown here.

Picture Plane

Fig 1

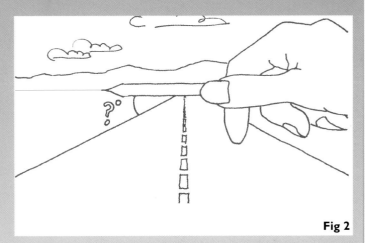

Fig 2

The picture plane is the name given to the surface upon which you intend to paint (or draw). This is perhaps best imagined as an enormous sheet of clear glass upon which you have traced the image which you see through it (Fig 1). In this book the picture plane means initially the paper upon which you have designed the project (the scale of the image having been reduced) and then the wall or panel upon which you paint (in which case the image may appear the size you have observed it to be).

All the elements which are affected by perspective and which in the end appear on the picture plane are drawn in blue. Black lines which appear on the picture plane have not been affected by perspective – by this I mean the outer edges of the painting.

If you can find a quiet, straight road, stand in the middle of the road and look straight ahead of you, holding a pencil horizontally at arm's length at your eye-level (Fig 2). You will notice that the sides of the road appear to converge in the distance at your eye-level.

You may also be able to judge the angle between your pencil and the sides of the road. Learning to judge angles like this will help you to draw.

Try imagining now that you have an enormous sheet of glass in front of you (as shown in the diagram) and could place the horizon at your eye-level as a horizontal straight line. If you could draw the side of the road on the glass you have already begun to appreciate and understand the relevance of perspective in design.

Key
Black lines: *elements in real life, including edges of painted 'opening'*
Red lines: *eye-level*
Blue lines: *imaginary elements*
Green lines: *important 'construction' lines*

Central Vanishing Points

Fig 1

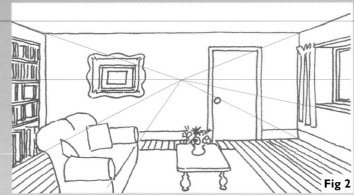

Fig 2

All lines which are parallel to the direction of view appear to converge to a point on your eye-level. Try this with a straight road. If you are lucky enough to have found a road which is flanked by buildings, or a fence or indeed anything constructed with edges parallel to your feet (as you look along the road), you will notice that all lines parallel to your feet appear to converge at this one central point in the middle of the horizon, i.e. at your eye-level (Fig 1). This point is known as a central vanishing point.

In the case of buildings, the edges parallel to your feet form only part of a line to this point. Lines which are vertical stay vertical and horizontal lines perpendicular to your own direction of view stay horizontal. If you do not have access to a long straight road, try standing in the middle of a reasonably uniform room. Face one wall, square-on and in the middle of it. Notice that the lines which form the edges of the floor and ceiling and which are parallel to the direction of your feet also appear to converge at an imaginary point on the wall facing you (Fig 2). To check this out, hold some long straight sticks in front of you and adjust the angle until they appear to follow the edges of the floor and ceiling to a meeting point in the middle of the facing wall. This is the vanishing point for these lines if we were to draw them on the picture plane. The photo of The Arches on the left shows how important vanishing points are in making an illusion work. For the methods used here, see pages 122-124.

Other Vanishing Points

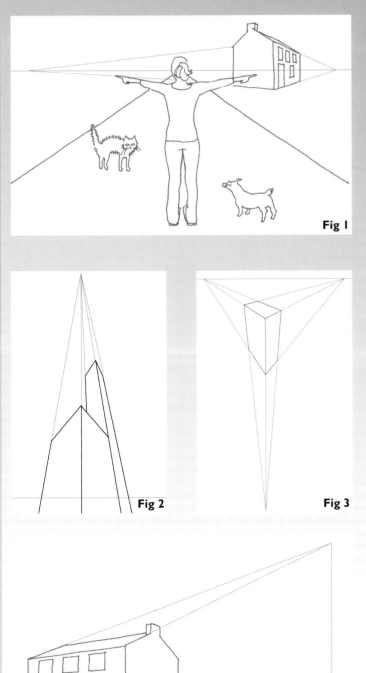

Fig 1

Fig 2   **Fig 3**

Fig 4

All sets of parallel lines, whether in the drawing of buildings, furniture, open doors or any other objects in your design, have their own vanishing points. Although the objects may be set at different angles to you, most of the vanishing points will be on your eye-level. These can be located in real life by looking in the direction parallel to the sides of the object in question and throwing an arm out parallel to the sides of the object and pointing towards the eye-level (Fig 1).

Vertical lines usually stay vertical unless you want to exaggerate height, or if your direction of view is up or down. In this case there will be another vanishing point way up in the sky if you are looking up at a very tall building (Fig 2), or, conversely, deep underground if you are looking down from the top of a very tall building (Fig 3). This is called three-point perspective – see page 24 for more details.

Parallel sloping lines (e.g. pitched roofs) don't have a vanishing point at eye-level. Any sloping lines on the same plane (e.g. sides of a sloping roof) appear to recede to a vanishing point on a vertical line above or below the vanishing point on the eye-level where the sides of the building appear to meet (Fig 4).

Key		
Black lines:	*elements in real life, including edges of painted 'opening'*	Red lines: *eye-level* Blue lines: *imaginary elements* Green lines: *important 'construction' lines*

When you are looking through magazines for ideas, try to guess the position of the camera that took the photo. The eye-level is also the horizon in a flat landscape, but so often the actual straight horizon is obscured by trees, buildings or mountains which might rise above the eye-level.

There are many visual 'experiments' you can try without much effort. Try standing in the middle of a (quiet) straight road as shown on page 19, and assessing the angle between the side of the road and the horizon. If you have any problems judging angles, try looking at them through a clear plastic protractor, making sure that the base line of the protractor is lined up with the horizon (you will have to hold the protractor upside-down).

During your 'experiment' you will have noticed that the sides of the road definitely seem to converge to a point at your eye-level. This is called a vanishing point and it is also important to be aware of this while designing a mural as, again, it affects your drawing.

All lines which are parallel to the direction of view (pointing in the same direction as your feet as you face your subject – in this case the picture plane) appear to converge to a point at natural eye-level. So far, we have simplified this to mean only the sides of a straight road if you are standing in the middle of it, but paintings would be rather boring if we just looked at straight roads or paths, so have a look at pages 20 and 21 to see how vanishing points may affect a more complex subject.

In real life, objects are not always conveniently placed with sides that are parallel to the direction of view, so artists can be helped by understanding what happens when the object you are looking at is set at an angle to the direction of view. (See page 21 – Other Vanishing Points.)

Going back to the scene we set before (i.e. standing in the middle of the straight road), a building set at an angle to the road will have two sides visible, the edges of which appear to converge to different vanishing points not in the centre of the view. The important fact here is that these points still lie on the natural eye-level. It's possible to 'eyeball' (i.e. guess the position of) these other vanishing points approximately by throwing out an arm in a direction parallel to the sides of the building and then pointing to the eye-level as shown in the drawing. If you had an enormous sheet of glass placed in front of you, you could theoretically mark these vanishing points on the eye-level. Because buildings are cubes, there would be one vanishing point in a direction parallel to one side and another in a direction parallel to the other side, both being located at eye-level. Finding vanishing points can be done in a technical way – this is shown on page 26 by using the projection method to do a perspective drawing from a plan.

After making yourself aware of all these ideas, you might be forgiven for wondering why they are relevant, but now you can use all of this knowledge to make a proper drawing in preparation for your mural. It's almost impossible to control the painting on a large scale without first planning your design on paper. When you do start to paint, you will know exactly where you are on the wall.

Making a scale drawing

To make a more accurate drawing, begin working in scale. For this it is helpful to have a scale ruler (see page 44) which converts measurements from their realistic value down to a manageable size for your drawing. Because they remain correctly proportional to each other, use the scale ruler to measure distances between elements in the scale drawing, and convert back to life-size to draw on the wall. You can estimate measurements by using a tape measure and 'eye-balling' the

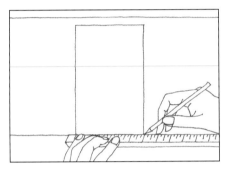

size of things, e.g. to guess the size of a window, measure the space you think it should occupy full-size on the wall.

If you have not got a scale ruler, you will have to be more mathematical and do some sums to help you represent the real measurements on paper. For example, to draw at a scale of 1:20, 1 cm on your drawing represents 20 cm, or if you prefer to work in imperial measurements, ½ in represents 10 in (i.e. 20 times the size of the drawing).

On the right I have shown the beginning of the drawing for The Arches (see page 120). To start your design, first draw the shape of the wall to scale on your paper showing the ground line and the top of the wall. Draw a straight line across the shape to show the eye-level. This, you can measure in the scale you have chosen from the ground line. I usually use a scale of 1:10 or 1:20. Now fit your ideas into the space, considering whether you intend to look down on things or up to things.

Plan and Elevation

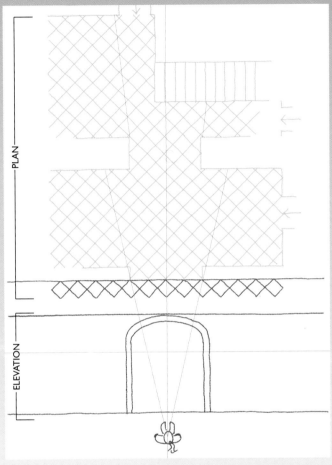

A plan is a bird's-eye view setting out the viewpoint in the real world, the picture plane and an aerial view of the imaginary features, shown in blue. An elevation shows the wall as you would see it if you were standing in the position you have shown in the plan. These are usually drawn to scale and positioned on paper with the elevation directly below the plan. (See also page 17.)

Key
Black lines: *elements in real life, including edges of painted 'opening'*
Red lines: *eye-level*
Blue lines: *imaginary elements*
Green lines: *important 'construction' lines*

Once you have the shape of the wall to scale on paper, overlay pieces of tracing paper to manoeuvre the various elements into their positions, starting with the 'opening', if there is one, through which you wish to look at the 'view'.

Do you want buildings to seem close or far away? How far above your eye-level are the distant hills? When drawing any building in the distance be aware of your own relationship to it, e.g. if you are on level ground looking at a building in the distance, your eye-level will appear to be about two-thirds of the way up a ground-floor doorway in that building. This will help you to locate the building itself in your design.

Using Vanishing Points

Now you can start to use vanishing points in your design. Lines drawn towards vanishing points on the figures appear in green as these are the 'construction lines'.

One-point perspective

One-point perspective is when we have just one vanishing point – this is often all you need for a good trompe l'oeil painting. This means we have chosen a point – usually dead central on the natural eye-level – to which all lines which would be parallel to our own feet, as we face the picture plane, appear to recede. This might mean lines forming the corners of an opening (e.g. a window or a door), or the upper and lower edges of books on a shelf (see page 130).

Try this on a drawing, adding in the shape of the wall and the eye-level (to scale), then choose a point central to your viewpoint and, using a ruler, draw the lines representing the

corners of an opening pointing towards this vanishing point. You will be amazed at how whatever you are drawing begins to make sense. It gives the drawing a feeling of depth. If you look at the Tuscan View (page 62), A Cornish window (page 98) or The Arches (page 120), you will see how drawing the lines correctly in the corners gives the work more depth.

Obviously, as you look at a recess containing a door or window, the upper and lower corners will have different angles from each other when pointing towards a central vanishing point as the angles are affected by your eye-level. It's these differences that are important to the illusion.

Two-point perspective

A design will have more than one vanishing point (as shown in the 'experimental' drawings on page 21) when you wish to show objects set at different angles to the direction of view, for example in the diagram on the facing page, where you might wish to show an open window, or in the case of the open doors in the Tuscan View painting. The plan and elevation drawings on the facing page show the difference between one-point perspective and two-point perspective.

Three-point perspective

If you want to exaggerate the height of a building you are looking up at by making the vertical lines go to a vanishing point high in the sky, or conversely make it seem as if you are very high up by making lines go towards a vanishing point deep underground, then you are drawing three-point perspective. This is shown on page 21.

One-Point Perspective

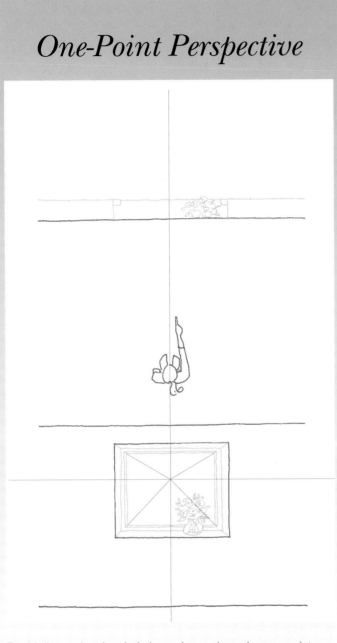

The bird's-eye view (or plan) shows that we have chosen a point, usually dead central, to view the painting. From this viewpoint, all lines which would be parallel to the direction of view (i.e. parallel to your feet) appear to recede to a central vanishing point on the eye-level. This helps to make the corners of the opening look convincing.

Key
Black lines: *elements in real life, including edges of painted 'opening'*
Red lines: *eye-level*
Blue lines: *imaginary elements*
Green lines: *important 'construction' lines*

Two-Point Perspective

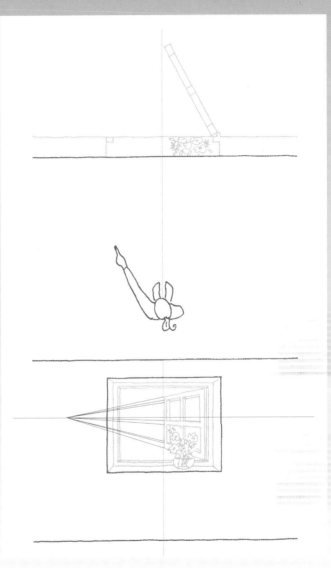

Again, in the bird's-eye view (or plan) we have a central viewpoint. Although we still need the central vanishing point for the corners of the opening, this time the open window has a vanishing point of its own which we can 'eyeball' by pointing in a direction parallel to the open window. The vanishing point for the open window will be found on the eye-level in the direction we pointed. This is called two-point perspective. The top and bottom edges and glazing bars of the open window appear to converge at this point. Finding these vanishing points in a more technical way is described on page 26.

Using the Projection Method

Although most murals can be designed using only a basic understanding of eye-levels and vanishing points, you may wish to extend your skill to include making a perspective drawing from a plan by using the projection method. (Page 122 shows a more complex example.)

Here, I wanted to create an open window through which I could look down on to a beach, and the painting was to be positioned behind our kitchen sink to liven up a plain wall.

I 'eyeballed' the distance I would stand from a similar real open window so the angles at the top and bottom of the real window did not appear too acute (try this to see what I mean), and in order to work out how much 'view' I would like to see. Looking through a clear protractor held upside-down helps to visualize the angles which you can then sketch either on paper or on the wall in chalk.

Experimenting with a real open window also helped me to decide how open I wanted my painted window to be. I established my viewpoint by trial and error, and wrote down the distance I would theoretically stand comfortably from the picture plane (i.e. 3 m/3¼ yds). I opted for opening the window to 70 degrees from the angle of the picture plane as this gave me the correct amount of view outside.

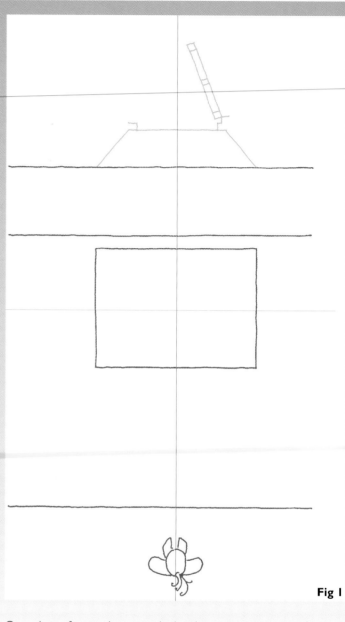

Fig 1

On a piece of paper, draw to scale the elements you are sure of, choosing a scale suitable for the size of the paper. On the upper part of the paper draw a bird's-eye view (or plan) of the imaginary opening set in the wall (this can be worked out from existing openings in the building). Draw in the open window, matching measurements to a real window. Add your viewpoint to the plan by experimenting with an open window. I stood 3 m (3¼ yds) from the picture plane. Below the plan, using the same scale, draw an elevation of what you know, i.e. the ground line, eye-level, width and height of the opening (Fig 1). Don't worry if the position of the viewpoint gets muddled up with the elevation – just remember it relates to the plan.

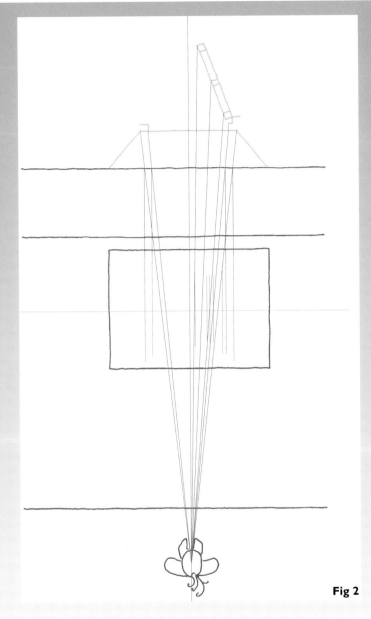

Fig 2

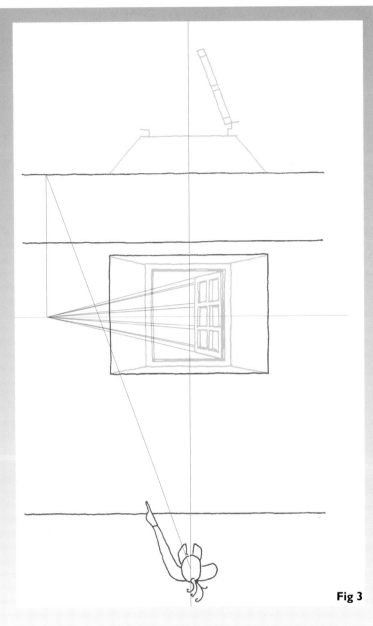

Fig 3

Start to connect important points in the plan (e.g. the edge of the window, window frame, etc) with the viewpoint below, as shown. Where the 'connection' crosses the picture plane, draw a vertical line downwards into the elevation, as shown (Fig 2). This will give you the positions of all the vertical lines in perspective. These lines would be in a different position if the viewpoint changed.

Key
Black lines: *elements in real life, including edges of painted 'opening'*
Red lines: *eye-level*
Blue lines: *imaginary elements*
Green lines: *important 'construction' lines*

Remember the arm pointing towards a vanishing point parallel to the sides of a building (see page 21). In the same way we can find the exact position more accurately. Draw a line parallel to the open window up to the picture plane in the plan and vertically down to the eye-level in the elevation below. The point where it touches the eye-level is the vanishing point for the top and bottom edges of the window and the glazing bars.

The window has another vanishing point for the pieces which show the thickness of the window. This is a long way along the eye-level and can be found in the same way (i.e. draw a line parallel to those edges from the viewpoint to picture plane and down to eye-level).

To find the back edge of the window sill, connect the viewpoint to that point in the plan, cross the picture plane and bring the line down to meet a line from a matching position on the picture plane (as if it were full size) to the vanishing point (Fig 3). This works exactly as the floor tiles on page 30.

Applying projection method to other designs

Going back to the design for the Tuscan View (see page 17), we would now be able to draw the French doors correctly and confidently. We could draw a plan, showing the picture plane – our wall. We would set out steps one to three, as on pages 26-27. On the plan, put in the door frame and angled doors, deciding on the angle of the opening. We would refer to our first 'intuitive' sketch to make this decision. You will soon discover that standing very close to an open door produces very acute angles between the door frame and the top and bottom of the door. If your protractor is transparent, you can measure this angle by looking at it through the protractor itself. You can then compare this with the angle you sketched. Open doors and windows look less alarming if you stand further away, although you may find that you don't have enough room to get back to a comfortable viewing distance – so cheat!

To find the vanishing points for the open doors, remembering that each door has two – one for the top, bottom and all the glazing bars, and one for the other edges as shown on page 27. Follow the same steps as for the window on pages 26-27. Draw a line parallel to the door drawn on the plan, from the viewpoint, up to the picture plane and vertically down to the eye-level. This locates the vanishing point for that edge of the door. Because the door has a thickness (which I hope you have described on your plan to scale) you will then draw a line parallel to that edge from the viewpoint to the picture plane and down to the eye-level. You will find that one vanishing point (the first) is quite close, and may be within the drawing itself, and that the other one is some distance away, outside the drawing. You may have to tape extra paper to the side of the drawing to locate its position.

Before drawing the doors, look at the opening – in other words the hole in the wall wherein the doors and door frame exist. Everything can be drawn using exactly the same system as before. Take the back edge of the wall (in the plan) towards the viewpoint. Where this line crosses the picture plane, drop it vertically and you will find the position of the back edge of the wall in your projection on the elevation.

To find out what happens to the bottom and top edges of the opening, simply head towards a central vanishing point on the eye-level from the ground line and from the top of the opening as it is in the real world, in other words, life-size. The point where you cross the vertical line which shows the back edge describes the depth of the wall in perspective. This works in the same way for the doorframe, and having done this you will be ready for the door itself.

The vertical edges of the doors can be found using the same system (i.e. from viewpoint to relevant point in plan, across picture plane, then vertically downwards). Now you can use the vanishing points to draw the doors properly. If the doors look strange, your viewpoint is too close.

Practise this by doing projections of straight-forward shapes and architectural features. You will soon master this and achieve convincing realism in your work.

To Summarize

1 Using sensible guesswork as a guide to size, lay out a plan using a suitable scale (ideally 1:10 or 1:20), positioning features as you want them to appear. Show clearly the picture plane and extend it out to the sides.

2 Underneath the plan draw an elevation to the same scale centred on the centre of the plan showing the ground line, height of the wall and width of the opening and adding the eye-level which should also be extended out to the sides.

3 Position the viewpoint on the plan marking it clearly.

4 Connect the main points in the plan with the viewpoint and project them down vertically to find their new position in the elevation.

5 Locate the relevant vanishing points by drawing lines parallel to edges shown in the plan from the viewpoint up to the picture plane and project vertically down to meet the eye-level.

6 Complete the elevation.

7 Measure the reference points on the drawing and convert them back to full-size to position the elements on the wall.

Common Perspective Problems

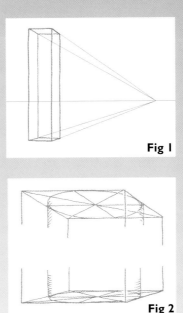

Fig 1

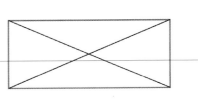

Fig 2

Using the vanishing point and the eye level, it helps to imagine a column as square (Fig 1). Then use diagonals to divide the square as shown (Fig 2). A circle touches the four sides in the middle of each side and is much easier to position and draw like this. It gives the top and base of columns (or, for that matter, anything else with a circular top or base) a much more convincing shape.

To find the perspective centre of a square or rectangle (e.g. the side of a building), use the vanishing point, then the diagonals. The area can first be halved, then quartered, and so on (Fig 3).

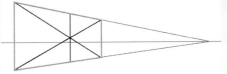

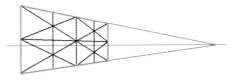

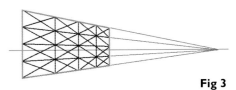

Fig 3

Other Ways of Spacing in Perspective

How do you work out spacing in perspective? This is relevant to all equally spaced objects receding from your viewpoint, e.g. books on a shelf in perspective or square floor tiles receding into the distance.

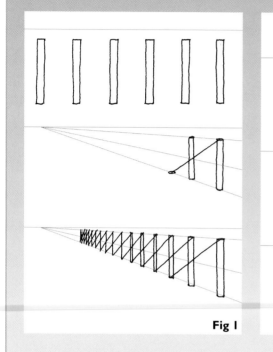

Fig 1

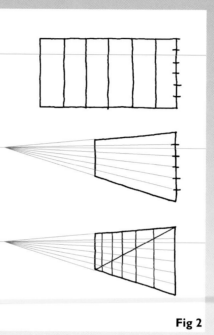

Fig 2

Fig 3

To find the position of the next post (or column, or anything vertical receding into the distance), a simple exercise will do it. First, draw two lines, one along the top, one along the bottom, converging at the vanishing point. Next, draw a line halfway up the post (or whatever it is), which goes through the middle of the next post. (This, too, will head towards the vanishing point.)

Now draw a line from the top of the first post through the centre of the second post to join the lower line. This intersection is the position of the third post, and so on (Fig 1). It works the same on a flat surface when you want to show equally spaced horizontal lines receding into the distance.

A rectangle (e.g. the side of a building) can be divided into equal horizontal parts using the same number of divisions as you want verticals. Draw a diagonal and note where it crosses the horizontal lines. The same method can be used when the side of the box is drawn in perspective, i.e. when its edges and the drawn horizontals go to the vanishing point, the upright divisions will be correctly positioned by the diagonal.

The principle is always the same: divide the area into equal parts, draw a diagonal which links opposite corners, and where the diagonal crosses the horizontal lines (Fig 2) you can position the vertical divisions..

By drawing the horizontal divisions proportional to the spacing you require, this method also works with unequal spacing.

By dividing horizontally and then drawing lines to the vanishing point, you can use a diagonal line to give you the correct spacing in perspective.

To draw floor tiles, draw a line showing the picture plane, a plan above it to scale showing the floor tiles, then add the viewpoint (your position in relation to the wall). Below this, set out a ground line and add the eye-level (usually 1.5 m/5 ft). Mark on the ground line the real size of the tiles, then draw lines to the central vanishing point from these marks. Draw a line (shown in green) from the viewpoint in the bird's-eye view to the back edge of the tiled area. Where this line crosses the picture plane, connect it vertically downwards to meet a line on its way to the vanishing point in the elevation, as shown (Fig 3). This point shows the back edge of the floor area from that viewpoint and that eye-level. Now you can use a diagonal to position the horizontal joints in the tiles.

Shadows and Reflections

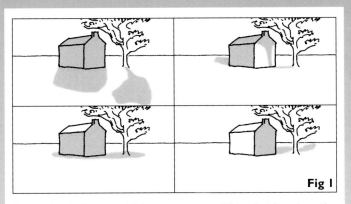

Fig 1

Even at the design stage, it's important to establish a feel for where the light is coming from. Try to imagine the sun's rays (which are parallel) have been blocked out by the shape you have drawn (Fig 1). This is best perfected by observation rather than complex technical methods.

Try to practise looking at shadows cast by objects (Fig 2). Having an awareness of shadows in your memory will help you to achieve a three-dimensional illusion.

Fig 2

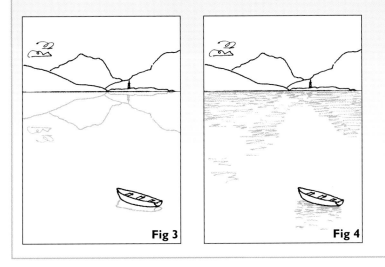

Fig 3

Fig 4

Shadows

It's hopeless trying to be too technical about the perspective of shadows, and yet they play such an important part in trompe l'oeil painting. A shadow can really describe the space around an object.

The shape of a shadow is best learnt by observation (Figs 1 and 2). Make yourself look at the strange shapes that the sun's rays make as they pass a form on their way to the ground. The sun's rays are almost parallel and all you have to do as a painter is to hold in your mind an idea of where the light is coming from and what shape it might make as the object in question blocks out these rays. Of course, there are technical ways of calculating exactly how shadows work, but these are very complicated. It's far easier to learn simply by looking, and then by trial and error.

Reflections

Like shadows, you can learn to look at reflections and use your experience in a painting – with wonderful results. Water always reflects something, whether it's just sky, or buildings, trees, boats or bridges reflected upside-down on the surface.

Calm water reflects an image like a mirror, although it may be discolored by the water (Fig 3). Rough water breaks up the surface (Fig 4) and here, it is worth remembering that the water has become sectioned into triangular blocks (i.e. the waves rising up – page 109 explains this in greater detail). One surface of this 'triangle' reflects the sky or the landscape behind the water, while the other reveals the underneath of the water itself.

Preparation and Equipment

Like anything in life, things can be done 'on the cheap' or you can spend as much money and time as you have available to achieve the desired result. I subscribe to the view that when tackling any project it's a good idea to assemble the tools you already have and then add a couple of new things. I always recommend buying good quality brushes and paints whenever possible (cheap brushes fall apart, losing hairs and shape). Use paints and brushes you feel comfortable with, i.e. things that are easy to handle. Anything that intimidates you is best left alone (I often feel overwhelmed by very expensive brushes and end up not using them in case I spoil them!).

Look at the surface upon which you are going to paint and decide how best it should be prepared. Traditionally the painting would be done directly on to a wall, but it is also possible to paint on panels which can be 'made to measure' and fitted to the chosen wall space.

Preparing surfaces to paint on is almost as important as doing the painting itself. This trompe l'oeil was painted on the walls surrounding a swimming pool so, because the surface would be constantly splashed, I used 100 per cent acrylic paint. To add extra protection, the walls were varnished with clear 100 per cent acrylic varnish.

Painting on Walls

Painting on the wall in the room we are planning to enhance is the favorite option. We will have the feel of the environment, the scale of it, its natural light qualities and an idea of the perspective which will be easy to 'eyeball'.

The surface may have been painted in the past. It may be rough, unstable, damp, flaking or pitted. The paint previously used may not be compatible with the materials we intend to use in our trompe l'oeil. All these things need to be considered before we begin.

When confronted with a situation which requires expert advice, talk to a good decorator or seek help from a DIY shop. Give them the facts about the wall, the kind of punishment the surface is going to take and your own painting preferences, and listen to what they recommend. Experts enjoy sharing their knowledge. They are the sort of people who make the world tick, the sort whose knowledge passes down through generations like the paintings themselves. When in doubt, find someone who knows! Don't feign knowledge – it will only land you in trouble.

In an ideal world we would ask for a newly plastered fresh surface. The surface can be pink plaster (a color which I always think makes a wonderful base color for painting – see page 55), or a smooth cement render. A plaster surface is smoother and therefore kinder to brushes. Inevitably, there will be less natural texture on the wall surface which may be seen as an advantage or a disadvantage depending on your own individual preference. I love working on cement render as the surface has a little more 'bite' to it.

If working with a builder, ask him to produce a flat, even surface, completely free from damp. Really emphasize this point. A wall can be affected from behind as much as from the front, and in a way, modern paints are better suited to dealing with conditions which affect the surface we look at than the disorders which can affect the condition of the wall itself. No-one wants to spend time and effort on a painting which lifts from the wall after a short period. A wall which is exposed to the outside on the other side is also susceptible to damage from the elements unless properly sealed from the outside. Ask a builder for proper advice and don't be tempted to skip these stages.

A wall that has been plastered specially for mural painting must be allowed to dry out. This means that plaster or cement render should have time to let all water content evaporate. Nothing is more disheartening than spending several weeks working on what you believed to be a stable surface, and then having a crack appear from top to bottom through your painting. This is likely to happen with a new surface which has been artificially 'cured' with the help of a dehumidifier or too much heat. Do not start until sufficient time has elapsed (perhaps several weeks) for the natural drying of the surface. Remember the drying time will be longer in winter than in summer. It may be necessary to use a dehumidifier if time is of the essence.

Assuming that the wall has been correctly rendered and plastered, when you begin to paint, make sure that the air temperature in the room is high enough to allow the paint to 'go off' satisfactorily.

Preparing the surface

Unfortunately newly plastered walls are not always available to us, and we may have to make do with what we've got. Don't be put off! Beautiful effects can be achieved on the most irregular of surfaces. When confronted with a less than perfect surface, turn it to your advantage! Think of all the wonderful frescoes you have seen and admired. Think how marvellous an aged painting looks, with its faded or darkened colors peeling from the antique canvas. There's something mysterious and intriguing about it. Its history is shown in the nature of the deterioration, and that deterioration itself can be studied and exploited to help you to produce a fascinating mural. Incorporate the texture into your design and make the most of it. Try to see it as good fortune rather than bad.

It is important to stabilize a poor wall as much as possible, using products especially designed to seal and bond a surface, such as a water-based or acrylic sealer. As before, seek expert advice. Describe your surface in great detail and use the recommended products to prime the wall, making sure that conditions are suitable at the time for painting and priming.

If the wall has been previously painted it's important to find out about prior applications of paint. Limewashes must be removed as overpainting a limewash does not work. This

You can use the existing wall surface to your advantage, especially where you want the finished surface to look highly textured, as in this case. Where the wall has a rough surface, you must make sure that it is stable before you start painting, but the finished effect can benefit tremendously from the added texture.

can be softened then removed by a steam wallpaper-stripper. Painting in acrylic (water-based) paints on top of old oil paint also does not work. Either strip the wall completely, or continue to use oil-based paint, or find out about products which can be used to isolate the oil from future applications of paint. You can use a PVA or acrylic sealer here, painted on in thin layers.

Priming the wall

The wall needs to be primed with a suitable paint that will act as the base coat for the painting. Primers are either oil-based, in which case you want an alkali-resisting type, or water-based acrylic or non-acrylic. Because technology changes so fast, always ask the advice of an expert at the very outset.

Oil paints seal the surface of a wall, whereas acrylic paints allow the wall to breathe through the paint. Although I would not suggest that you paint onto a wall that is not completely dry, it must be considered that acrylic paints and emulsions will allow some flexibility if there is any doubt about the surface.

Diluting the first coat of paint is sometimes recommended by manufacturers, but be careful not to dilute the paint more than recommended as this will affect the adhesion to the surface.

My favorite primer is gesso, now sold in ready-mixed acrylic form (you used to have to boil rabbit skin to make it!), but the cost of it on a large project is often prohibitive, and emulsion paint would be a suitable alternative.

Applying paint

In general when priming a wall in preparation for your mural, there are some basic rules for applying paint to achieve a good long-lasting surface.

Paints are either oil-based or water-based, but the two types don't mix. It is possible to cover a water-based paint with an oil paint, but not vice versa. In circumstances where a wall has been painted with oil and you really want to continue in acrylic, you must thoroughly sand the wall to improve the adhesion. (Make sure that you wear a face mask whilst doing this as the dust from the old paint may be toxic.) After sanding, use a suitable primer on the wall before starting work.

On fresh plaster or a sand and cement render on normal interior walls, a thin coat of emulsion diluted 3 parts paint to 1 part water will suffice as a priming coat, and as you will see on page 55, this does not need to be white but can be a color chosen to help with your painting.

Walls surrounding swimming pools or exterior walls can be primed using 100 per cent acrylic sealer which is totally impervious to water.

Painting on Panels

As mentioned earlier, it is possible to paint 'off site' on made-to-measure panels which can then be fixed to the walls at a later date, assuming that you have the appropriate studio facilities to do the painting elsewhere.

As with walls, there are advantages and disadvantages to doing this. Clearly you are not so familiar with the

This trompe l'oeil painting of The Monk was done on a large panel of MDF (see page 95 for more details).

surroundings, working away from the actual situation, and therefore must go to great lengths to be sure of eye-levels and light sources which may affect the painting if the aim is to achieve a certain degree of realism. This is particularly important in dealing with perspective, when the viewpoint must be clearly understood.

Transport of the panels can be a risky business, although with expert packing and careful delivery (there are firms who specialize in the carriage of items like these), there is no reason why this should cause a problem. The size of the work must all be worked out taking into account entrances, doorways, staircases and hairpin bends. You must be prepared to repair damage caused in transit.

There are various methods of fixing rigid panels to the existing walls. You can use 'secret fixing' which is a little like the hook-and-eye system of doing up trousers! Countersunk screws can be used, the disadvantage being that some touching-up will be required to conceal the evidence. There are also very strong contact adhesives available – these are only recommended where permanence is assured!

The advantages of painting on panels may outweigh the disadvantages. You can move the painting in the future (providing that you didn't use the aforementioned contact adhesive, which is likely to pull the wall down as well!) and take it with you when you move house. You have a wonderfully stable surface upon which to work, one that can be beautifully prepared and primed, and perhaps the most important of all, you don't need to be in anybody's way while you paint it! If the area to be painted is very large, you may be able to conceal joints in the panels cleverly in the design itself. Quite often a mural may be part of other home improvements going on, and an artist deep in thought can be a very irritating obstruction to electricians and plumbers going about their business!

There are several different surfaces which are suitable for made-to-measure murals. My own preference is for MDF (medium density fibreboard) as it is very stable, rigid and robust. It comes in several different thicknesses and sizes, and can easily be cut to the exact dimensions required, although if cutting it yourself, you must be careful not to inhale the dust produced during the cutting. The drawbacks of MDF should be considered. It is susceptible to damage from damp unless completely sealed, so prime it on the back as well as the front, so that it is completely protected. Painting the back helps to prevent warping. It can also be damaged by impact on the corners. There is a slight possibility that MDF may have a limited life, although this is not yet known for certain.

Other portable surfaces include canvas and architects' drafting film, which I personally don't enjoy much as I find it too smooth. Canvas can be stretched as you would for normal painting, then cut to size and glued to the surface with contact adhesive (ask your art supplier how to do this). The trouble with canvas is that the larger the area, the more vulnerable it becomes to the damage during transport (it is usual to transport it rolled up). It also becomes rather awkward to stick on, as the larger it gets, the heavier and more limp it becomes. The canvas should be stuck on by an expert.

Priming MDF panels

MDF is best primed with two coats of acrylic gesso, rubbed down with fine sandpaper between coats. This gives a wonderfully absorbent surface, and can be improved afterwards by staining whatever color you wish, although you can buy gesso in a variety of colors.

When applying gesso, don't paint it on in neat square blocks, as you can already use the background texture to your advantage in the development of texture and added drama in your painting. Paint with criss-cross strokes, which later can be re-discovered by sanding the painting to enhance the texture. Always follow the manufacturer's instructions on the container, as they will help you to achieve a perfect result. Do not over-dilute primers as this will affect their adhesion to the surface.

Priming can be done with ordinary, good quality household brushes, but I usually use a varnish brush for this or a large domed continental brush.

Paints

Top of my list for quality, durability and ease of working are high-quality acrylic artists' paints, which are water-soluble, and environmentally-friendly in that the majority of them are not toxic. Personally, I have very strong feelings about protecting myself (and everyone else for that matter) from the harmful effects of chemicals which may be innocently inhaled or somehow digested while painting. It is a known hazard of using oil paints that one may be exposing oneself to harmful substances, both through inadvertently breathing in the toxic fumes of solvents such as white spirit and turpentine, and through skin contact with poisonous particles in the paint itself. If you do choose to use oil paints, ask your art supplier about low-odour solvents as there are other more recent inventions now on the market. Look carefully at warnings written on the side of tubes for

This trompe l'oeil around the swimming-pool at the Watergate Bay Hotel in Cornwall was painted using 100 per cent acrylic paint which is completely impervious to water as the surface would have to withstand constant splashing. The surface was rendered with sand and cement, rather than plastered.

any alarming contents. Wherever possible, both for your own sake and that of the environment, choose paints which carry proper guarantees of safety.

My own preference is for the more expensive American acrylic paints as they not only have a far greater color range using very strong pigments, but they are also far easier to mix. They also stay 'wet' on the palette for an unbelievably long time.

There are mediums available to add to the basic paint in order to slow down the drying time. These are called retarders. The cheaper varieties of acrylic paints can be heavy in texture and more likely to change drastically in color as they dry. They can also dry too quickly on the palette during painting. Inevitably one uses more of the cheaper paints, so spending a bit more initially tends to be

cost-effective in the long run. Start by buying 60 ml tubes, increasing your quantity with your confidence. You will almost certainly need more white than any other color.

There are also glazing mediums, which allow you to dilute the paint to an almost transparent consistency whilst still maintaining its adhesion to the surface, so that you can overpaint a color and change it very gradually, or change only part of the whole area.

If you do not have access locally to a major art materials store, try using mail order. Some of the larger firms are very quick to send their products when you order from a catalogue, and may turn out to be considerably cheaper than the local shop.

Although, in general, murals benefit from the use of artists' quality materials, I have painted walls with all sorts of different paints. For example a large indoor swimming pool with a sand and cement rendered wall could be painted with pure acrylic household paints specially designed to withstand constant contact with water. Some paints are even designed to be used underwater. It may be necessary in your project to consider fire regulations. If you are going to be working in a public area, you must consult the local authority. They will put you in touch with the fire officer to advise on all fire regulations, which are very strict but do tend to change. Never embark on a commission without checking these regulations, as neglecting to do so could land you in terrible trouble in the future.

Although, as previously mentioned, I try to avoid using traditional oil paints, it's not always possible to do so, perhaps because the walls have already been painted with oils. In this case, artists' oil paints are perfectly acceptable, and can be encouraged to dry overnight with the addition of a few drops of a liquid drier or a modern lead-free drier to the mixing medium. This is a substance used in commercial oil paint to make it dry quickly. You can buy it from a reputable paint or hardware store.

Diluting paints

In this book I describe techniques used to paint murals with artists' acrylic paints. They are very adaptable and can be applied in thin or thick layers. Immerse the brush in water and then mix the paint, adding more water gradually until it is the consistency of thick cream. Paint that is to be flicked with a toothbrush (see page 56) should be more watery.

Paint can be diluted until is is almost just a tinted water. If you want to stain an area of your painting, add a very small quantity of color to a mixing medium.

Varnishing

Although these paints do not really need varnish for protection, I think they benefit from a couple of coats of a suitable clear acrylic matt or semi-matt varnish. This helps to even out the slight differences in the shine in different colors and also enhances the overall look of the painting.

This strange-shaped painting was painted to look as if it had been revealed beneath subsequent wall painting by scraping away the contemporary paintwork! It was painted in oil as previous layers of paint were oil. I added a few drops of a liquid drier to the mixing medium to help it to dry overnight. See page 78 for more details.

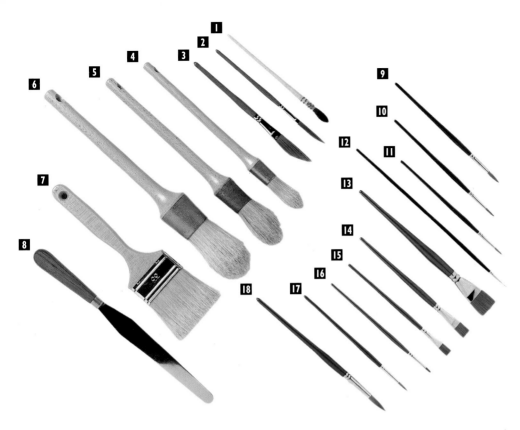

1 Small squirrel wash brush (ideal for clouds etc)

2 Small sword-line brush (for very fine lines)

3 Large sword-line brush (for fine lines)

4, 5, 6 Domed natural hogs' bristle brushes (for covering large areas quickly)

7 Flat natural bristle brush (for priming and varnishing)

8 Palette knife (for all sorts of uses!)

9, 10, 11 Sable round pointed brushes (for detailed painting)

12 Extra-fine sable round pointed brush (for very small details)

13, 14, 15, 16 Flat synthetic brushes (my favorite general purpose brushes)

17, 18 Round pointed synthetic brushes (also general purpose brushes)

Brushes

Brushes are so personal. All I can do, if you are not already a painter, is to suggest what I like and hope that you will experiment and learn which ones become your friends and which ones end up being used for mixing the paint! It's always worth looking at what other people are using and experimenting wherever possible.

I always seem to end up using the flat, square-edged brushes which are generally used as wash brushes. These are soft, one-stroke brushes. I love their versatility. They can quickly cover the surface when used flat, and are so precise and neat when used on edge. I find I can paint a whole mural with so few brushes. I start covering huge areas with a round continental-style hog's bristle brush, and then move on to a small selection of flat wash brushes. All the fine detail is added using sable watercolor

brushes, with the occasional very fine lines put in with sword-line brushes (see page 103).

Watch out for cheap brushes as they always lose their hairs and are a false economy. No one will think any the worse of you in a shop if you try to pull the hairs out of a brush that you intend to buy! If the hairs are easily dislocated from their holder at their base, don't buy the brush, as it will also leave its hairs all over your painting!

Brushes must be washed immediately after use (and during use), as the paint dries very quickly and, once dry, cannot be removed, except with paint remover.

Alternatives to brushes

I also use a lot of other things to apply the paint, including old toothbrushes, dishcloths, floorcloths, paint rollers and all sorts of different sponges, both natural and synthetic. The

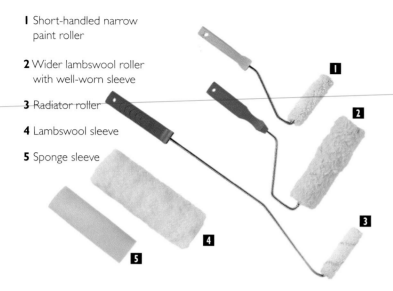

1 Short-handled narrow
   paint roller

2 Wider lambswool roller
   with well-worn sleeve

3 Radiator roller

4 Lambswool sleeve

5 Sponge sleeve

actual uses of these things will be further discussed in the chapter on painting technique (see page 48).

Radiator rollers (the sort with long handles that are used for painting behind radiators) are an invaluable asset as they are light and effective.

Other Useful Equipment

When I finish painting a trompe l'oeil, the amount of equipment that I have actually used during the work amazes me. So much of the equipment is domestic or home-made and yet has proved useful time and time again.

Stepladder: a good, strong, modern aluminium stepladder. Don't be tempted to use your grandfather's old wooden thing dragged out of the garden shed! Ladders can be lethal, especially when you are concentrating on what you are doing. A low step is also invaluable.

Scaffold: for bigger projects, invest in lightweight kit that can be assembled and dismantled easily and has wheels with proper brakes for safety. Proper flooring for the tower should also be used, not planks that stick out too far and cause accidents. This equipment can often be rented.

Boxes for storing paint and equipment: plastic stacking boxes are ideal.

A paintbox/toolbox: I have one with a drawer which lifts out with suitable compartments in it for brushes, etc.

A chalk line: available from hardware stores, this is a steel pear-shaped container housing a reel of string which can be wound in and pulled out, and which also contains powdered, colored chalk which impregnates the string as it is wound in. Because it is heavy, it also acts as a plumb-line, giving you a certain vertical for your starting point. All lines drawn at right angles to this first vertical line will thus be horizontal. To make long straight lines using the chalk line, the string must be pulled tight through measured points, then 'pinged' (picked off the surface and let go quickly), leaving a perfectly straight chalk line. This is invaluable for horizons and architectural drawing requiring lots of lines as the method is so quick and accurate. Over large distances, an assistant is useful to hold the other end of the string (you can use masking tape to hold it if no one is available).

A right-angled triangle: in my toolbox I have a plywood triangle with the right-angled edges about 40 cm (16 in) in length, the third side being at 45 degrees to the other two. It has a wooden handle attached in the middle. This has proved very useful for many years, because so often you want to know when a line is a true horizontal or vertical, and providing that you already know one, this quickly tells you the other.

A straight edge: made from 2 cm (¾ in) quadrant (round-edged wood), with a handle attached to the flat side, and 90 cm (36 in) long, I rest the brush on this when painting a straight line. Rather than splodging the paint under a ruler, if you paint *away* from the straight edge, and up to your previously drawn straight line, you get a cleaner result. The roundness of the wood further prevents smearing the paint.

Stainless steel shield: a sharp piece of stainless steel set in a plastic handle made for protecting skirting boards when wall painting. I find this useful for masking off edges, although it does need constant wiping. A straight piece of Formica or Perspex will also do the job.

Compass: I have a huge compass that holds chalk and can draw circles up to a radius of about 90 cm (36 in). Available from school equipment suppliers, it is surprising how often I use it (e.g. when drawing an ellipse). Use a pad of masking

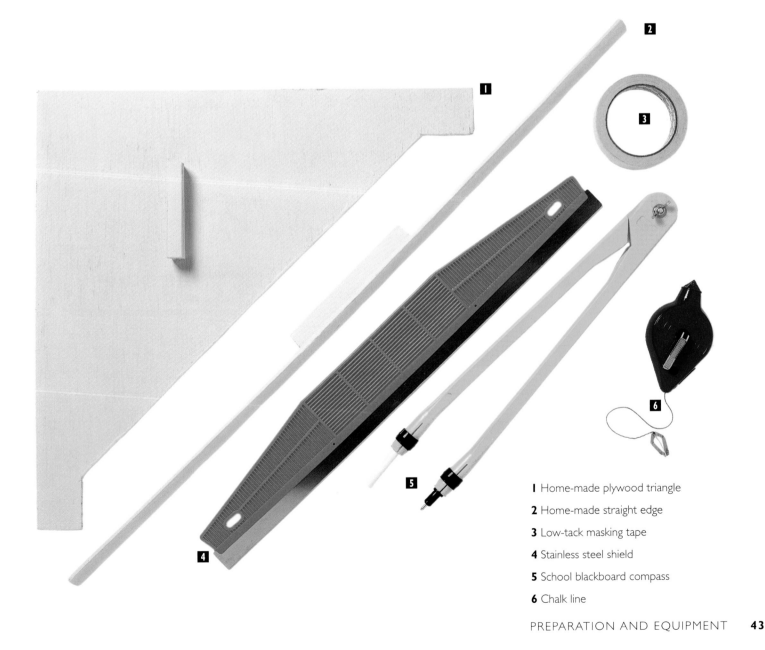

1 Home-made plywood triangle
2 Home-made straight edge
3 Low-tack masking tape
4 Stainless steel shield
5 School blackboard compass
6 Chalk line

tape under the needle to stop it damaging the surface.

A tape measure: essential when planning the trompe l'oeil and transferring the design to the wall.

Overhead projector: this is an expensive item which is not essential, but if you are going to be doing a lot of work, you will find it a wonderful tool for transferring your designs to the wall, correcting drawing mistakes and even for trying out something without actually making any marks on the wall. My projector is the kind found in schools and colleges, and projects images from acetates. These acetates can be drawings or tracings or even prints and photocopies on acetate. The size of the image can be adjusted by changing

the distance of the projector from the wall. See page 58 for more information, but watch out for distortion which can be minimized by making sure that the lens height is central on the wall.

A long steel rule, preferably at least 1 m (1 yard): this is easier to handle for measurements once you have made all your key marks with the tape measure, with the added bonus of being able to use it for drawing lines.

Scale ruler: a ruler which converts life-size measurements into proportional manageable measurements which you can use on your drawing. For example, if you were using a scale of 1:20, then 1 cm on your drawing would represent 20 cm

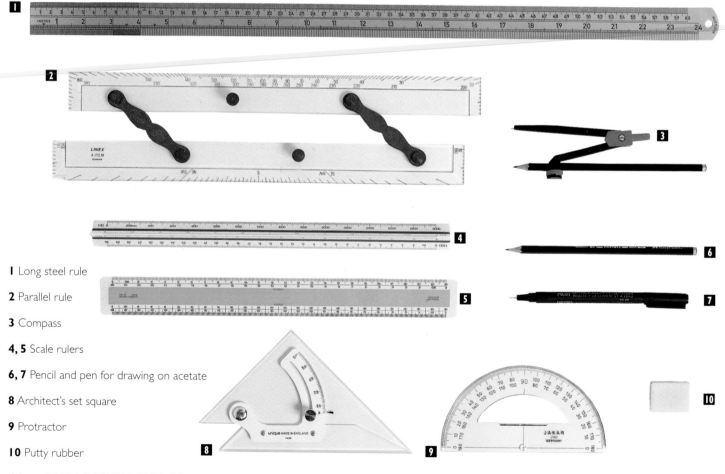

1 Long steel rule

2 Parallel rule

3 Compass

4, 5 Scale rulers

6, 7 Pencil and pen for drawing on acetate

8 Architect's set square

9 Protractor

10 Putty rubber

Spray Equipment

Depending on your level of competence you may like to consider using this in your work. Spray equipment consists of an air compressor – different sizes and capacities are available. I have two – a small one which is very irritating because it doesn't switch itself off when it reaches full pressure, and a larger, more complicated one which has a capacity of 8 cubic feet per minute. I have a full range of different spray guns, ranging from a tiny airbrush, to a huge one which I use for covering large areas very quickly. This large one has a remote pressure system, which means that the spray gun is not actually attached to the pot containing the paint, which has two advantages: firstly that the weight of the paint is not in your artistic hand, but carried in the other hand, and secondly that you can spray ceilings without the paint running down your arm.

For most murals, if I include spray work, I use a small gun with a quarter- or half-litre paint pot. It is vital to follow the manufacturer's safety directions, and always remember that sprayed paint travels further than you think it might! Spraying paint can be used for covering large areas but also for making really subtle gradations of color or creating beautiful aerial perspective by using a fine dottle (a uniform mist of tiny dots of paint) of paint as a misty effect. To do this you use a very low pressure. Increase the pressure for a solid spray. All the equipment must be cleaned regularly to prevent blockages.

By diluting color to the consistency of thin cream, and straining it through a fine mesh, all water-based paints can be sprayed.

Using the air compressor and spray gun on an extremely low pressure produces a 'dottle', which can be used to tremendous advantage in the following way: first establish the distant horizon (i.e. line of hills, mountains or whatever), having already painted the sky in several shades of suitably blended color. Next, dottle over the distant horizon, using the lowest sky color. Move nearer to your viewpoint and paint more landscape (hills, trees, etc.) which will be sharp against your first hills. Dottle again. Your distant landscape will recede further away from you visually as it receives more covering from the spray, and the nearer hills will also be diffused.

Repeat this, painting the landscape, dottling, painting the landscape, and each time you do it the distant hills recede further into the lowest sky color and you 'drop' sky in front of your hills. It's the most wonderful way to create natural aerial perspective, giving almost photographic realism to your painting. If you haven't got spray equipment, you do pretty well on a small scale with a carefully controlled toothbrush! To 'smooth out the wrinkles' in the sky colors using the spray, just dilute the sky colors and spray one overlapping the other until a perfectly smooth 'bond' is created. For more information on aerial perspective, see page 54.

Additional interest in this landscape/sky relationship can be achieved with an overspray with a contrasting pink/orange dottle, which can add a ray of sunshine to the painting just where you need it.

in real life, or 1:10 means 1 cm represents 10 cm. (The imperial equivalent of 1:10 would be 1 inch representing 10 inches, and so on. Remember not to mix metric and imperial measurements, as conversions are usually rounded up or down for ease of use.) Using a scale ruler saves a lot of complicated maths. Because they remain correctly proportional to each other, you can also use a scale ruler to measure reference points on your drawing and convert back to life-size.

Protractor: for measuring angles.

Pencils: for sketching.

Pens for drawing on acetates: permanent or water-soluble pens for drawing on acetates for overhead projectors. Choose very thin varieties.

Putty rubber (eraser): the best type for erasing pencil marks.

Sponges: I use them to create interesting textures and to make paint look like stone or other rough surfaces. I always look after these very carefully, making sure never to allow paint to dry on them as they are expensive.

Dishcloths/floorcloths: my favorite variety is the 'stockinette' kind that garages use. Once you have tried using cloths like this to enhance textures and give you a new feel to your paint, you'll learn to spot your favorite ones on supermarket shelves! They are all slightly different. An affordable luxury for artists!

Rags: don't throw away old T-shirts any more! Cut them up into manageable sizes and add them to your kit for mopping up, along with old cotton sheets and tablecloths (natural fibres are more absorbent).

Toothbrushes: useful to flick diluted paint at the work (see page 56). All toothbrushes seem to behave in a slightly different way, so don't throw away old ones!

Masking tape: this comes in different widths. I use wide and narrow. Masking tape is marvellous for lots of things, from holding the other end of the chalk line to securing chalk on the end of a brush handle for drawing at arm's length. It can be used for its true purpose as well – to mask off areas needing protection from paint (used in conjunction with newspaper, whole sections of the painting can be covered). A low-tack tape is safer on your painted surface. (N.B. There are lots of masking fluids and films on the market and if you are going to be doing a lot of masking, it would be worth familiarizing yourself with the latest products. I use

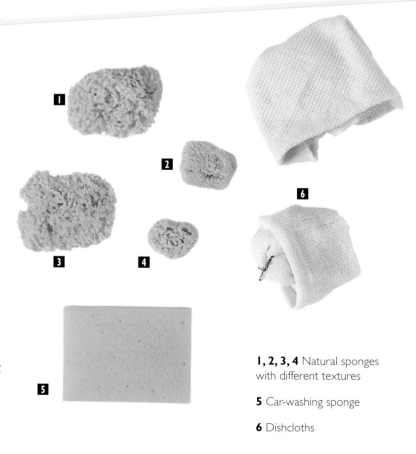

1, 2, 3, 4 Natural sponges with different textures

5 Car-washing sponge

6 Dishcloths

Transpaseal, usually used for covering school books, with very satisfactory results – cheap and reliable!)

Scissors, Stanley knife and scalpel: for making stencils when required. Make sure the blades are sharp.

Screwdriver: for opening tins of paint.

Containers for mixing: delicatessens and restaurants will be happy to part with plastic tubs in every size, often with lids. You can also re-use film cannisters, tins, yoghurt pots, ice cream cartons and jam jars. If you must, buy containers in art shops but this doesn't have the same environmentally-friendly feel to it.

Sticks for mixing paint: I use 30-cm (12-in) lengths of thin dowel (the type usually used for building kites).

Palette: for a small painting, an ordinary palette or board will do. Going up in size you might like to think in terms of using a palette with compartments like a tray for baking buns. Larger still and you will need to mix colors in containers which should be airtight, e.g. empty paint tins.

Palette knife: for mixing paints on the palette.

Clingfilm: useful for preserving paints on the palette or for covering mixing containers. In the absence of clingfilm, use plastic bags, or use the lid of an ice cream box as a palette and cover the lid with the box when you stop painting.

Tracing paper: I usually use a whole pad during each mural.

Layout paper: cheap paper you can scribble on and not feel that you are wasting it! Any scrap paper will also suffice.

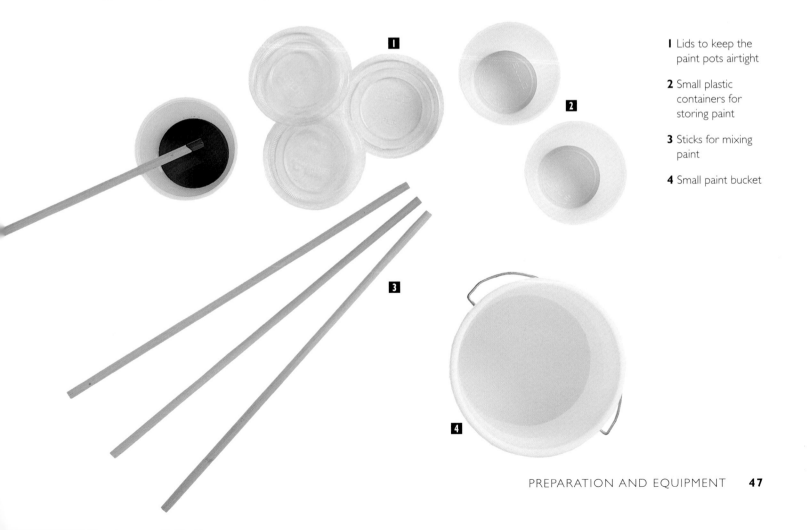

1 Lids to keep the paint pots airtight

2 Small plastic containers for storing paint

3 Sticks for mixing paint

4 Small paint bucket

Painting a Mural

Start by organizing yourself properly. Assemble your drawings and any photographic references you may have collected. Keeping them out of the way of dripping paint and yet always visible requires careful thought. See-through plastic folders are a good way of protecting pictures you are looking at. If you have found your references in expensive books, have some good quality color photocopies made before you accidentally ruin the book. Spread all your reference material out on an old table to one side.

Put down suitable floor protection in case of spillages and tape it down around the edges, with an extra layer where you will be mixing paint. An old piece of hardboard would be good, or another table, for mixing paint on. On the floor I use dust sheets or polythene sheeting because it's waterproof. You can also use old bed sheets or curtains. A visit to a jumble sale or a recycling centre is cheaper than buying new stuff!

In this painting I projected the image on to the wall. The trouble with using an overhead projector on this scale is that your own composition may be lost and unexpected distortion can occur. If you do use a projector, it may be better to sketch out the subject freehand first in a faint color to decide the size and position of the image.

Using Colors

Lay out your colors so that they are conveniently displayed to you. It's very annoying to have to rummage for colors when you are concentrating on the painting. As you gain experience you will discover which are your favorite colors, but to begin with I suggest that you use the range shown on the right. Whatever the scale of your project, and whatever sort of paint you plan to use, you should be able to achieve a good range with these basic colors.

These are the names given to colors in some of the American and British paint ranges, but for a project where you are using say household emulsion paint, check the names of these colors on an acrylic paint index against an index showing the range you want to use.

Using the color index

Look carefully at references for color guidance, either something you can observe for real or a well-printed photograph. If you have in front of you some photos showing the mood that you are looking for, half-shut your eyes and see if you can tell whether there is background warmth in the shot. By this I mean whether warm colors are present, e.g. pinks, oranges, yellows, browns, because this will guide you towards a suitable color for the background. You don't need to use the same picture as the one from which your composition is drawn. Just find one which has the right kind of color (even if you used a particular photo during the designing of the composition of the mural you may be able to improve on the color by looking at another photo). If

you stare at the picture for some time you will be amazed how you gradually become more conscious of the colors.

This is where the DIY color index comes in handy. The more colors there are in the index, the better. Simply 'match' areas in the reference to selected parts of the photograph, and then make a note of your choice in pencil on the index or stick a note to it. The idea here is to mix up color exactly as it is shown in your reference. For a small project you can do this as you go, hoping that you can repeat it when required, but mixing larger quantities for a bigger painting and keeping the paint in airtight containers will be worth the time spent doing it.

You can do this as many times as you have the patience for, the principle being that the greater the range, the more realism you will have in your painting. This will help to isolate the color and make it easy to identify. Start by picking out just a few obvious areas of color that are easy to see, like different parts of the sky. Complexity will develop with practice.

As an exercise, try observing colors in this way in real life. Ask yourself to solve questions like 'what color is the road in front of me, both in the sun and in the shade?'. You will be very surprised! What color is the grass just outside my window, and further away into the distance? And what about the sky, just above the horizon and higher up? Try sorting out the different shades of a 'white' window frame – the surface that faces you, and the edge that points inwards and catches the light. You will find that one side is probably a different color from the other, and by shutting one eye and holding

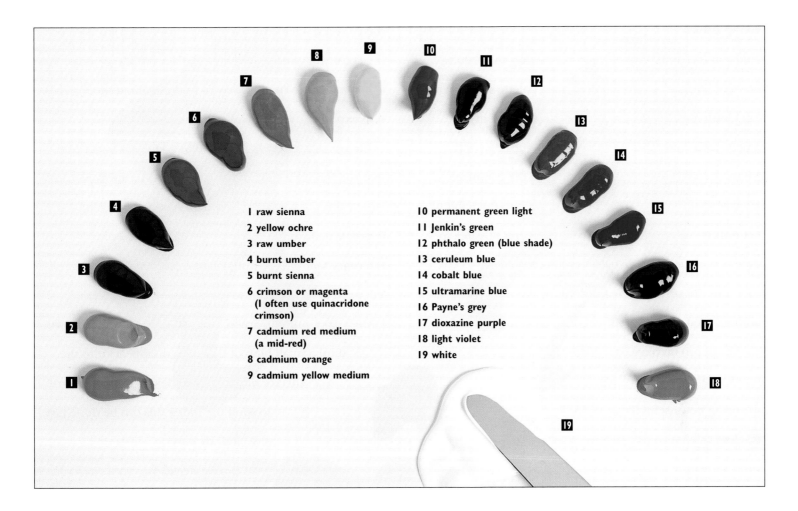

1 raw sienna
2 yellow ochre
3 raw umber
4 burnt umber
5 burnt sienna
6 crimson or magenta
  (I often use quinacridone
  crimson)
7 cadmium red medium
  (a mid-red)
8 cadmium orange
9 cadmium yellow medium

10 permanent green light
11 Jenkin's green
12 phthalo green (blue shade)
13 ceruleum blue
14 cobalt blue
15 ultramarine blue
16 Payne's grey
17 dioxazine purple
18 light violet
19 white

the color index at a comfortable distance in front of you, you can flick through until you find exactly the same color. Make notes on the index in pencil so that you can rub them out later. If you haven't got an index, lay a piece of thin clear plastic on top of the photograph you are using and mix paint until a blob of it 'disappears' into what you are looking at, in other words it's a perfect color match.

Make sure that the light on the color chart is similar to what you are looking at. It's no good trying to find the color of a lovely blue sky by looking at it from inside a room. You have to take yourself outside and allow the color index to be exposed to similar light conditions to that which you

are looking at. This will help you to research all the colors you will need to begin your painting and really understand the way one color affects another.

In this way you will learn to find out about the color of objects and, believe me, you will be amazed how all your previous ideas will be swept aside and how a new awareness of color begins to grow.

All this may seem remarkably pedantic, but it's so much easier to paint when your palette contains the right ingredients. It's just like cooking. You can't possibly produce cordon bleu cuisine unless you prepare the ingredients properly before you start! It really is worth the effort.

If you are painting larger areas, spending time mixing up all the colors you might immediately need before you start will give you immense freedom to just 'get on with the job'. Acrylic paint can be stored in airtight containers for days, weeks or even months. Again, when working on a larger scale, take the lids off all the available colors to give yourself the best chance of accuracy which might only be possible with the addition of the tiniest bit of something quite unexpected.

Mixing sky colors

As children, our first paintings have blue sky at the top and green grass at the bottom. We tend to leave the middle blank because we haven't thought about that bit! Later we paint the sky down to meet the landscape at the horizon, but consider this. We stand on the surface of the landscape in the sky. As the landscape upon which we are standing recedes away from us into the distance, more sky interrupts our view of it, and affects the color we perceive as we look at it. It may help to imagine this as layers of gauze. (This is known as aerial perspective – see also page 45.)

This is very important to mural painters because the tremendous depth which we want to describe in our painting, and which is the whole nature of painting trompe l'oeil, is, in essence this perception of changes in color. The sky itself is more dense nearer the horizon (more layers of gauze) – it is actually quite grey with a strong hint of magenta. (Try the color index and look at

the observed result.) As you look upwards, the sky thins and the color we observe changes through various shades of blue. (This is because outer space is as black as ink, but when diluted by several miles of atmosphere, either damp or dry, depending where you are, this black becomes the beautiful blues that we know and love.)

If you can pick out four shades of sky color from either real life or your photographic reference, moving upwards from the horizon, and use these to paint the sky in your mural, you will already be halfway to doing a spectacular painting. Your findings will also show that the sky is not simply a straightforward mix of blue and white, but a complex mixture of ultramarine blue, perhaps burnt sienna or magenta, maybe pthalo green, Payne's grey and white (see page 52).

Try some observations downwards from the horizon, matching the colors very carefully. Doing this correctly will give you the latitude you need to paint realistic sun-drenched hillsides, white buildings, ploughed fields or whatever else you want because the effect of having a properly observed sky color is to allow the white buildings or washing on a line or whatever else to leap forward towards the onlooker.

So often I have seen paintings which intend to show sunshine, but fail miserably simply because the sky is too bright and too light and there is no 'room' to show sunshine which needs contrast in order to exist. When the sky is the correct color (which will be surprisingly dull and dark if properly done), buildings can gleam forth,

When you have found a color that appeals to you, use the color index to identify it. Making notes in pencil on the index means that you can choose all the colors for a project before you start painting.

trees can be bathed in sunshine. The amazing thing is that the sky appears in the end to be a very bright blue even when it is not. So many times people have commented to me on the richness of the blue sky in one of my murals, but it's really just an illusion!

Painting the Background

I usually start with a background color which I use to stain the area to be painted. This is in order to replace the terrifying sterile whiteness of the primer with a more comfortable disrupted surface which will not intimidate me. Another advantage of working on a background

which is not white is being able to show areas of light quickly, giving you more confidence in the overall feel of the painting. Later, as you continue to paint, you may find this original color coming through to the surface in places to give you a glow from underneath, which is why choosing the color carefully is very important.

Painting the background colorwash

Washing means diluting the paint with significant amounts of water to give a thin consistency. Using a diluted warm color of your choice, attack the wall! Enjoy it! Let yourself go! Using the biggest brush you have (I use a 2 cm (¾ in) domed

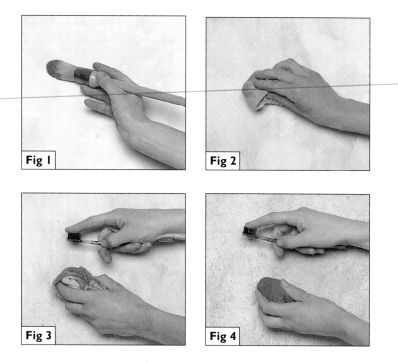

Fig 1

Fig 2

Fig 3

Fig 4

round hogs' bristle brush), make textures and patterns, especially in areas where you want to avoid flatness (Fig 1).

Dab the surface with a dishcloth, sponge or roller. Move paint around. Put it on and take it off. Let the surface develop a life of its own (Fig 2).

It has been said that every square inch of a Rembrandt painting is an abstract painting. This is what we want – the surface upon which we intend to paint to come alive. Try splattering the paint with toothbrushes (Fig 3).

You might splatter the surface with one color, dab it with a dishcloth (Fig 4), then wash over it with another color, keeping within the range that you observed earlier. Try contrasting colors – pinks and greens, browns and yellows. Try colorwashing several colors, one on top of the other. Try rubbing the surface you have painted with some fine sandpaper, so that you rediscover the original base color in places which will enhance the overall texture.

Rag-roll one coat (i.e. paint it on, then roll it off by rolling a screwed-up, absorbent rag over the surface), splatter another coat with an old toothbrush, wash another, then dishcloth another, keeping the same effect over the whole surface if you can. Don't worry too much if you can't manage this! It won't matter in the end because all of this background will be covered up by the actual trompe l'oeil painting, but this first familiarization makes you comfortable with the surface.

Textured areas will have natural depth and will show the intricacies of fine detail where you want them. So many times I have done this and almost stopped short of doing the mural itself because I have discovered some amazing paint effect, worthy of a wall-covering in its own right. If your courage fails you, try out the 'background' first on a spare piece of board before touching the wall.

Ideally the wall surface will end up being a uniform, if textured, surface upon which you can begin to paint. Even at this early stage you may like to paint a darker wash over the 'interior' parts of the painting, which will immediately give you a feeling of the 'outside' being much lighter.

Sketching freehand with a very faint, diluted paint which can easily be wiped off gives you a feel for the composition which may not be accurate, but is intuitive and can guide you when you are ready to draw more accurately by other methods to confirm proportions and difficult shapes. Don't worry if you make mistakes as it will all be covered in the end.

Transferring the Design to the Wall

Now you must decide how you are going to put your idea on the wall. Somehow one intuitively feels the right position for the arch, the doorway or the life-size figure, but it's so difficult to control the correctness of the shape on this scale. We need some reliable help here to give us confidence.

Squaring up

If you haven't got an overhead projector and don't wish to use scale (see page 23), square up your design. You can use a chalk line to help with the squaring up on the wall. If you've got colored chalk (I usually use bright blue), it will show up perfectly well on your background. This will guide you accurately, as to the position and proportion of everything and can easily be washed off afterwards. Use thin paint only slightly different in color from the background, so that a faint image appears.

Frame your drawing in a box of the same proportions as the wall you will be using (e.g. if your wall area is 5 metres/ yards by 2.5 metres/yards, then frame your drawing in a box which has the proportion of 2:1. (If it seems complicated use a calculator.) Work on a piece of tracing paper over-laying your drawing to avoid spoiling your original drawing.

Next draw straight accurate lines from corner to corner diagonally. This will immediately give you the centre, as it will on the wall if you put in the diagonals. This is your first important landmark. Draw lines through the centre, parallel with the top and bottom and parallel with the sides. Now

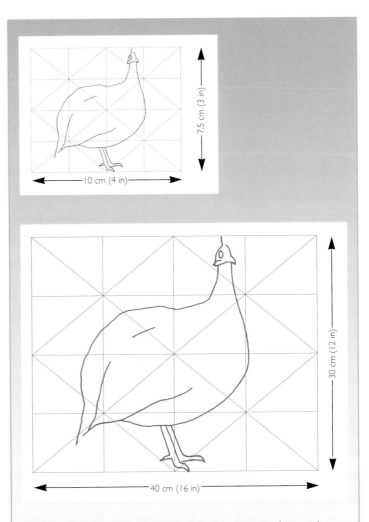

Draw a box around your drawing of the same proportions as the wall space, e.g. if you want the guinea fowl 30 cm (12 in) high and your original drawing is 7.5 cm (3 in) high and 10 cm (4 in) wide, the enlarged version height and width would both be four times greater, i.e. 30 cm (12 in) × 40 cm (16 in). Divide the box around the drawing in the same way as the box on the wall, first diagonally from corner to corner both ways to give you the centre, then vertically and horizontally through the centre and continue as shown. The shape of the outline which appears in each triangle on your drawing is easy to repeat in the larger triangles. Remove any chalk with a damp cloth.

your drawing will be divided into four equal rectangles, all bisected by a diagonal from corner to corner. Draw from corner to corner the other way in each rectangle. Now each rectangle will have its own centre, and you can join the new centres vertically and horizontally, which will give you sixteen rectangles, again each with their own diagonal. Draw from corner to corner again and then subdivide again. You can carry on doing this as much as you like, even focusing on rectangles that have particular interest for extra subdivisions. This simple method saves all the traditional measuring into squares.

Providing that the wall has the same proportions, which it will have if you have measured correctly and drawn the frame round your drawing accurately, you can now subdivide the wall in exactly the same way, using the chalk line if possible, or just draw straight lines if you haven't got a chalk line. An important tip here is to start marking out the wall from a plumb-line, i.e. a central vertical line drawn with the chalk line, or any piece of string with a weight on it, as almost all walls, floors and ceilings are surprisingly crooked, especially in older houses. You don't want your painting to end up lopsided.

Each triangle or rectangle in your drawing contains information to be transferred to the same space on the wall. If there are lots of triangles, number them on the wall and the drawing to guide you.

Using a very dilute color similar but not quite the same as your background color, start painting the design. Use a fairly fine brush. Be gentle and feel your way around softly. Strong, dark colors are difficult to conceal and are also too final when changes may well be needed. By using a color only slightly different from the background shade, any mistakes will not be obvious! A faint image is sufficient for you to stand back and survey. It's easy to obliterate, to change, to digest.

If you've kept the first painting subtle, it's easy to overpaint. You can use stronger colors as the painting develops.

Using an overhead projector

If you have access to an overhead projector, now's your chance to try it out. Trace the design carefully on to acetate, giving yourself as much information on the acetate as you can. Put the acetate on the screen. As explained on page 58, you could use tracings from different photographs or drawings, in which case you will need to do some juggling around with the distance of the projector from the wall. You don't need all the information on one acetate.

Subdued lighting will allow you to override the freehand image, while still being able to decipher the original composition, which is very important as it will guide you better than the projector as to the size of your subject and a natural composition. You may take some time to mess around with the position of things. Don't be afraid to go back to the drawing board at this stage. The design may not work first time, but this should not be seen as a disaster!

It is important to make sure that the lens of the projector is central to the wall to minimize distortion. This means you should place the projector on a suitable stand so that the image doesn't tip and become larger at its extremities. Distortion will still occur but you can take precautions to avoid it. Using a projector is very hazardous when it comes to architecture, and I always avoid it here because of the inevitable distortion, resorting instead to measurements taken from my scale drawing, or to squaring-up.

When using an overhead projector, be careful not to lose your own intuitive composition and watch out for distortion on a large scale. Set the projector so the lens is central in height and width to the area of the mural.

As with the squaring up method, sketch with quiet colors, just a little different from your freehand painting, using the former as a guide, and the new projected image as a confirmation. Don't be distracted by the inevitable muddle with the freehand attempt – it will all be covered up by the actual painting. Just build up a confident sketch. Switch off the projector frequently and look at what you have done.

Blocking in color

You can also begin to block in areas loosely, the sky for example. You may have to paint the sky several times, so the

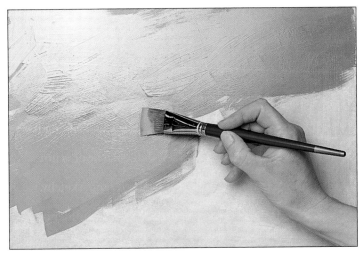

Get the sky blocked in (using carefully chosen and mixed colors) as soon as possible. It's exciting to see the effect of the sky color against the warm, textured background colors.

sooner you do it the first time, the better. The paint should be diluted with water or painting medium to a consistency similar to that of double cream, neither too thick, nor too thin. Try to estimate the quantity for several coats, but it is only experience which will help you to know how to do this. Even when the coats slightly vary in color, this can be to your advantage, because it gives an unexpected softness and quality to the work. The sky will appear as a wonderful color in comparison with your background, which it never could have done so immediately from a white ground.

Try to blend one sky color into the next, using a wide, flat, soft brush and dabbing it as you go with a damp dishcloth, but don't panic if this takes more than one attempt as acrylic paint dries quickly and this may be difficult. Using a clean, damp dishcloth to dab the paint as you paint it on with a brush helps to diffuse and blend it. Depending on the size of your painting, select the paintbrush that is easiest to handle on larger areas. You will see that several coats of thin paint give a more beautiful sky than one thick coat, especially when you notice the effect that the warm dappled background color has on the look of the final sky painting.

Gradually build on your drawing on the wall, keeping it loose and relaxed. Remind yourself that each layer is not yet the final one, and so feel free to keep it quite sketchy. Actually what you will be doing is building up confidence in your painting, and expanding the detail as you go. Let the painting develop.

Never expect perfect results immediately. Trompe l'oeil only really takes effect when all the different elements are in place, and when colors work together to give depth and illusion. It is the special relationship between one color and another which describes light and shade, warmth and coolness, and once the colors are contained in the right shape your mural will begin to look convincing, whatever the subject.

Using sandpaper

If you find part of the work begins to look flat, overworked or even just boring, try sanding it vigorously with some fine sandpaper. The resulting effect will be unpredictable, but will give you a new and unexpected texture which you can use to your advantage. You can also use sandpaper to exaggerate highlights, rubbing right back to the primer where necessary. Sometimes glazing thinly over the freshly sanded bit gives yet another interesting look. This sanding/glazing routine is perfect for painting rough stonework.

Developing the design as you paint

Happy accidents happen all the time. Mistakes have a wonderful way of becoming meaningful and attractive additions to your ideas, so don't panic when they happen. Don't feel locked into the limitations of the original design. It's only natural for your creativity to continue working, and you may find that things develop as time passes. I often find that although I have been guided by the original thoughts and design, lots of new ideas creep into the painting and add to the fun and to the feel of the whole work. When you do feel the need to make a drastic change, do experiment with the new idea on paper first (preferably a tracing laid over the original drawing), resisting the temptation to make wild, innovative changes on the wall without going through the design and perspective stage.

Try to keep the whole painting on the move at the same pace. Don't start to go into terrific detail in one part and abandon another, as you will ultimately find this very disheartening. It's better to go on being loose and sketchy all over and then begin to finalize the details.

Adding light and shade

The chapter on design and perspective (see pages 15 and 31) talked about light sources. As you paint now, keep the source of light fixed in your mind, so that objects in the painting are touched by light from the same direction. All forms can be made to look three-dimensional by establishing where the sun is and in trompe l'oeil we need

It is the effects of light and shade which really create the illusion of depth. This can be achieved using a combination of the right shape and carefully chosen colors.

to exaggerate this to create the extreme depth.

It makes sense to define as early as possible the areas in shadow (hopefully already done at the design stage). Colorwise, shadows are generally cold, and cold colors are best described by the addition of blue. As your perception of color increases, you may begin to notice reflected light present in the shadows. This is complex and can be daunting for the beginner, but with practice and concentration, you can achieve even more depth in the subject by hinting in the shadow some reflected light from elsewhere by flecking the cold color of the shadow with warmth, either with a sponge or with a toothbrush.

Use the color index to practise spotting the blue in shadows. It will give you pleasure once you can identify this blueness! Even at the underpainting stage, blue shadows contrasted with warmth (i.e. yellows, yellow ochre, red and crimson) will help to make the distinction between light and shadow. It is the effects of light and shade which really create the illusion of three dimensions and which give the painting real credibility.

Gradually your work will come together, and if you have enough patience to stick with it, and sufficient nerve to keep going through the 'uphill struggles' (which happen to everyone at all levels), you will begin to feel a tremendous satisfaction in a job well done!

Finishing Touches

The final stages of the work will involve intricate detail, and it is often this detail which 'makes' the mural into a true work of art. The onlooker will automatically be attracted to interesting and beautifully painted things, and may overlook large areas where not much is happening, although I recommend trying to consider at the design stage that all parts of your original drawing are going to be so much bigger on the wall that you must try to fill empty spaces!

Tuscan View

This painting was commissioned specifically to brighten up an ordinary kitchen wall, opening the wall out into a different time and a different place. During the long, wet winter months, the occupants of this house can gaze at the warm sun of a Tuscan summer's day, fondly remembering holidays spent in this beautiful part of central Italy.

I used pictures from travel brochures to plan the landscape, sourcing ideas from about a dozen different places. The peacock is my own, and he tends to creep into a lot of my paintings. I find

him hard to resist and he adds a certain exotic quality to the design. In some ways I prefer him to be still like this, rather than making his usual noise outside my studio door! The owners were delighted when I suggested including their dog in the mural.

PAINT

Burnt sienna
Cadmium red
Yellow ochre
Cadmium yellow
Payne's grey
White
Raw umber
Jenkins green
Dioxazine purple

EQUIPMENT

Large domed hog's
  bristle brush
Soft cloth
Toothbrush
1 cm (½ in) flat
  brush
Medium sandpaper
Fine pointed brush

The Stone Floor

Getting the perspective right for this floor is very important as it leads into the view beyond the stone terrace. Refer back to page 30 in the chapter on design and perspective for further guidance on this subject.

As this large and detailed trompe l'oeil took several weeks to complete, I painted the scene on to a large sheet of MDF (medium density fibreboard) so that I could work in my studio rather than on site. When the painting was complete, the sheet was set flush into a specially prepared recess in the kitchen wall. I then had to match the floor in the painting to the real floor in situ. Page 36 provides information on preparing and painting on panels.

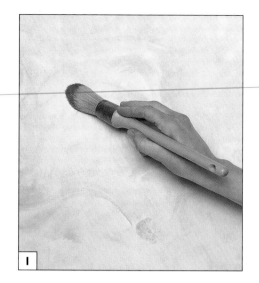

1 Begin by preparing the background color with a wash of burnt sienna, cadmium red, yellow ochre and cadmium yellow. Roughly apply a diluted wash on to the surface with the large domed hog's bristle brush.

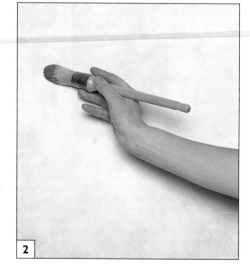

2 With the same brush, blend all the colors together using a free, swirling motion. Let yourself go and enjoy the paint!

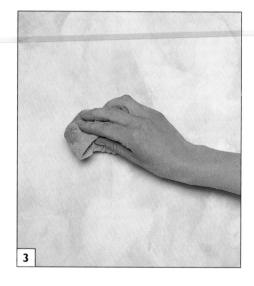

3 While the paint is still wet, fold a soft, clean, damp cloth into a small pad and dab the surface. This softens any harsh lines created by the brush and ensures the background colors are well blended. Leave to dry.

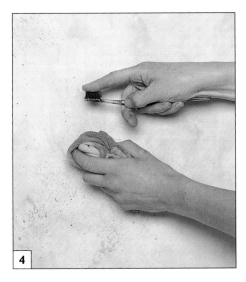

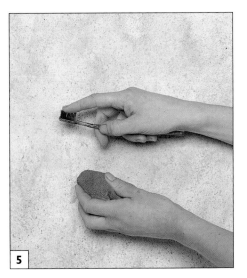

4 Using a toothbrush, flick some contrasting colors on to the dried wash, dabbing the surface with a cloth to blend the colors and to produce more texture.

5 Keep repeating the previous steps, gradually building up the color and texture until you achieve a 'gritty' look. This preparatory work can take some time as you need to allow drying time for the paints. You can speed this up with a hair-dryer.

6 After sketching the slabs with very faint lines, start blocking the slabs in with a flat brush (remembering that lines parallel to the direction of view all go to the central vanishing point). Use slightly varying shades of warm greys created with burnt sienna, Payne's grey, white and yellow ochre.

7 Using a fine sable brush and a mixture of Payne's grey and raw umber, work the paint in to the 'cracks' between the slabs, varying the thickness of the line as much as possible.

8 When the paint has dried, use a small piece of medium sandpaper to rub gently over the work. This helps to exaggerate the texture and bring it to life. Don't rub too hard or you will remove the layers of paint and expose the surface behind.

9 Don't worry if the sandpaper removes some of the lines. Simply paint them in again with deeper colors, such as Jenkins green mixed with dioxazine purple, improving the detail of the painting all the time. Don't expect to achieve a perfect result immediately – just continue building the paint up in layers, making each stone slab a slightly different color from its neighbour.

PAINTS

Raw umber
Payne's grey
White
Yellow ochre
Burnt sienna
Jenkins green
Permanent green
  light
Dioxazine purple
Ultramarine blue
Cadmium red

EQUIPMENT

Tracing paper
Soft and hard
  pencils
Ruler
Craft knife and
  cutting board
Stencil paper (this
  can be made by
  priming
  cartridge paper
  on both sides
  with emulsion
  paint, but the
  bought paper is
  better)
Masking tape
Natural sponges
1 cm (½ in) flat
  brush
Fine pointed brush
Fine sandpaper

The Balustrade

It's always best to make a stencil for this kind of repetitive shape as it means you can continually reproduce the original shape of the stone pillars correctly and with the right spacing between them. The card stencil can then be kept for any future paintings requiring a similar balustrade.

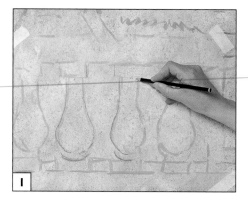

1 Tape a sheet of tracing paper over the sketched balustrade. Make a rough tracing from your full-size freehand sketch to establish the right size and general shape of the balustrade. Make sure the curves at the base look right for the eye-level – 'eyeball' this!

2 To refine this tracing, trace over again one half of the curve and mark the centre by ruling a faint line. Fold the tracing paper down the centre line and trace over the half-outline to make a complete pillar.

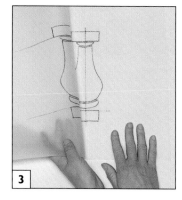

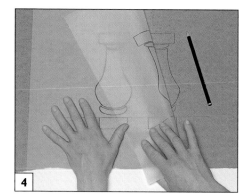

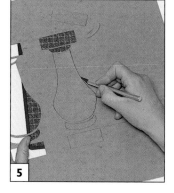

3 Fold the tracing paper down a centre line between the position of two pillars and trace over the first drawing to repeat the first shape exactly.

4 To make the stencil, first use a soft pencil to draw on the reverse side of the tracing paper over your shapes. Draw a straight baseline on the stencil paper and rest a matching baseline drawn on your tracing onto this line. Using a much harder pencil, draw over the tracing on the right side so that it leaves a print on the stencil paper.

5 Using a craft knife and cutting board, carefully cut out the two pillars of the stencil as shown, leaving pieces shown in step 6 to hold the stencil together.

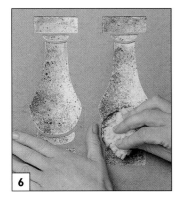

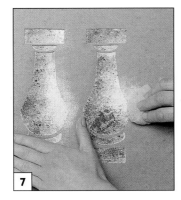

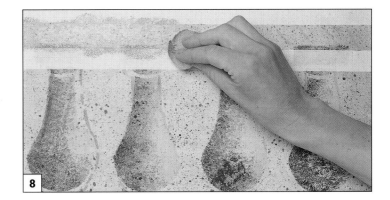

6 Stick the stencil to the wall with masking tape. You may need a pencil or chalk line on the painting to keep the stencil horizontal. Use a rough-textured sponge to dab a mixture of raw umber, Payne's grey and white in the shadowy areas.

7 For the lighter areas on the right, use a mixture of white, Payne's grey and yellow ochre and a finer textured sponge to apply the paint.

8 Remove the masking tape, move the stencil along by one pillar and re-tape it in position. This will give you accurate spacing. Make sure you keep it on the baseline. Use two strips of masking tape to make the areas above and below which are the coping stones and base and paint them in the lighter color, moving and resticking the tape to give you the shadow side of the coping stone in a darker color. Use different sponges to work from light to shade, keeping the direction of the sunlight fixed in your mind.

9 Now that you have an outline that you feel confident with, you can start to block in the background behind the pillars using a 1 cm (½ in) flat brush and a mixture of burnt sienna and Jenkins green.

10 Add the lighter green detail with a 1 cm (½ in) flat brush and a mix of permanent light green, white, Jenkins green, yellow ochre and dioxazine purple. You will find that using colors that contrast with the color of the pillars themselves helps accentuate the depth.

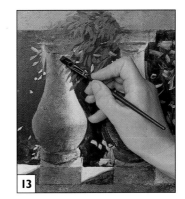

11 Using a fine pointed brush, carefully paint in the missing shadowy bits in a mixture of Payne's grey and raw umber.

12 It doesn't really matter what you do to make the balustrade look gritty. Flick contrasting colors, using the stencil to mask off the painted background if you need to. Try sanding with fine sandpaper and using different brushes.

13 Now you can start to paint the foliage falling over the coping stones at the top. This is done using a mixture of Payne's grey, raw umber, ultramarine blue, Jenkins green and yellow ochre and a 1 cm (½ in) flat brush.

14 Add the flowers in a mixture of dioxazine purple, cadmium red and white, using a fine pointed brush. Bear in mind that they are in the shade, as the light is coming from the other side of the balustrade.

PAINTS

Full palette of
colors (see
page 51)

EQUIPMENT

Fine pointed brush
8 mm (⅜ in) flat
brush

The Dog

When planning this part of the
trompe l'oeil I used my camera as a
design tool, looking down on the
small dog in real life as I would in
the finished painting. When taking
reference photographs of the dog, I
positioned her and the camera
carefully to make sure that the eye
level was correct. I wanted her to
appear as if she was looking out into
the garden. I also made sure that the
'sunny side' of the animal was the
correct side, i.e. the right, so that I
could paint in shadows accurately.

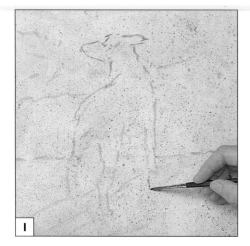

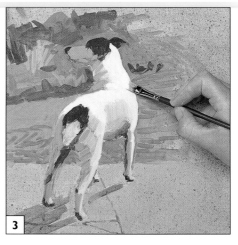

1 Using your reference, start by sketching an outline using the fine pointed brush, with a color only slightly darker from the background color but still visible. You can do this freehand, using an overhead projector or by squaring it up (see page 57).

2 Loosely paint the dog using a full palette of colors and an 8 mm (⅜ in) flat brush. Start to describe areas of light and shade and add a few vague details – there is no need to be too precise at this stage. For the lighter areas of her coat I used Payne's grey, white and yellow ochre; the dark patches were Payne's grey, raw umber and white. It helps to keep the whole painting together if you make other areas work around the dog to see things in context.

3 Remember that the white French doors are the most important aspect of the mural and to allow them to dazzle above all else, we must not get too bright anywhere else, so add a hint of Payne's grey and yellow ochre to the 'white' bits of the dog. She will still appear white. Use the smaller brush to paint detail and continue building up the roundness of the dog, working from light to shade and back again.

PAINTS

Full palette of colors (see page 51)

EQUIPMENT

Fine pointed brush
8 mm (⅜ in) flat brush
Toothbrush

Tuscan Village

I found a suitable picture of a village on a hill in a travel brochure. You could make an acetate from your reference photograph and project the village if you are doubtful about the composition of it. The great thing about scribbling on acetate is that you can do it as often as you like until it fits where you want it to!

1 Working from your reference, begin with a very loose faint outline just roughly defining a few roof shapes and not worrying about any detail at this stage. This is just to help you decide on the actual position of the village in the landscape.

2 Using a full palette of colors and the 8 mm (⅜ in) flat brush, start to block in the main areas (for sky see page 112). Remember that keeping the sky much darker and duller than you would imagine is what is going to make the buildings gleam in the sun. You can use the color index to choose your main colors (see page 50).

3 Keep redefining areas of sun and shade with the angle of the sun fixed in your mind as you paint. This will help to make the buildings three-dimensional even though the shapes are simple. The same applies to the surrounding trees and bushes which fill in the spaces. Use the 8 mm (⅜ in) flat brush for all this painting.

4 Work deeper into the shadowy areas, mixing Payne's grey and ultramarine blue into the colors. Think hot and cool colors – sun and shade – and keep working from one to the other. There is not much detail in this but it's surprising how a simple idea can be developed in this way.

5 Using a toothbrush, flick some of the sky color over the hillside and village to soften the outlines.

Tabby Cat

Why paint a trompe l'oeil cat as if it was staring down into the bath looking for fish to catch? The answer is very simple – purely for fun! This is one of those small visual jokes that I refer to in the Introduction on page 6 – it is just meant to amuse the onlooker. I was flattered to find that not only the humans in our house were interested in the cat; all the dogs had a good look at it as well before deciding that it didn't smell quite right and failed to move.

I photographed this cat with the idea for the trompe l'oeil already clear in my mind, so I ensured I captured him at the right angle and used the resulting photos as the basis for my painting. The painting itself was completed in one session. When working quickly like this, it is essential to ensure that each paint application is dry before progressing to the next stage so that there is no danger of the previously painted layer lifting. Extending the tail on to the timber bath surround emphasizes the three-dimensional effect. A painting of this size is ideal for a beginner, as good results can be achieved in a short period of time.

PAINTS

Payne's grey
White
Raw umber
Burnt sienna
Yellow ochre
Cadmium orange
Cerulean blue
Violet

EQUIPMENT

Pencil
Small pointed
  brush
I cm (½ in) flat
  brush

Painting the Cat

Trace the outline of the cat on to the wall in pencil or with a dilute mixture of Payne's grey and white. To achieve the correct outline, use an overhead projector (see page 58) or enlarge the drawing on to tracing paper by squaring it up (see page 57), then rub a soft pencil over the reverse of the outlines and trace it on to the wall.

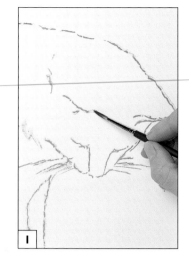

I Sketch in the outline of the cat, going over the initial pencil lines with a diluted mixture of Payne's grey and white. Keep the outlines pale as you do not wish them to dominate the finished painting – they are simply there to serve as guidelines.

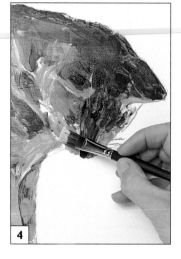

2 Using a flat-edged brush, begin to block in the main areas of color using a mixture of Payne's grey, white, raw umber and burnt sienna.

3 Using the same palette of four colors, continue to work on the background colors of the cat's fur. Work deeper shadows and darker areas of fur with a combination of Payne's grey and raw umber.

4 Begin adding lighter patches of fur and the stripes using a mixture of a little yellow ochre, Payne's grey and white. Gently blend the colors as you work but make sure they don't smudge together too much, resulting in a murky mess.

5 Complete the entire background of fur. Keep the painting 'rough' and simply try to cover the whole cat. Add a touch of cadmium orange if you wish to make the grey warmer. Don't worry about blending colors at this stage as any hard edges will be softened by added detail in later steps. When the background is complete, leave it to dry.

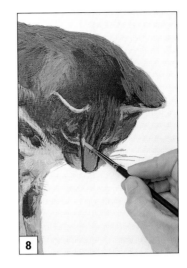

6 When the whole cat has been loosely blocked in, use a fine pointed brush to describe fur. The first coat of paint must be dry before you begin this stage or the paint will lift. Add white to Payne's grey and raw umber to make a shade of grey suitable for the paler stripes.

7 Continue using the small pointed brush and the same colors to build up the detail. Add more white to the mix for paler shades, and keep referring to your reference material to understand how the color of the fur gradually changes from light to dark and back again.

8 Paint in the cat's facial details using a light mix of white, Payne's grey and raw umber for the highlights and a darker mix with less white for the detail around the eyes and the nose.

9 Use a fine brush and a light mix of the three colors to paint in the detail of the fur on the cat's stomach. The fur here often sits in small clumps, so add this detail with short strokes of the brush.

10 Carefully add the whiskers using a fine sable brush and a diluted mix of Payne's grey and white. With a steady hand, draw the whiskers in one long stroke rather than several short strokes. This helps to achieve a clean, unbroken line.

11 Add the whiskers on the other side of the cat's face. Try to keep them the same shade as the set of whiskers already painted and make sure both sides are even in length.

12 The finished details are so important. The longer you spend on this stage of the painting, the more realistic the cat will be. Patience will really pay off in the end. Use short brush strokes to emphasize any areas of fur that require further detail.

13 Stand back from the wall and view the overall effect of the painting. Correct any details. Finally, touch up the wall around the cat using the original wall paint with a flat brush to neaten the edges of the trompe l'oeil.

Guinea Fowl

These guinea fowl have been painted sitting on top of the door frame and at other strategic points around the room. The point of painting them in unexpected places is the element of surprise and humor! A guinea fowl – a fairly comical bird in any case – would not normally be found perched on your doorframe, but therein lies the joke. It only works if you achieve a life-like quality with a clean outline.

Not very many people keep these birds, so I was lucky to have these subjects in my own garden to observe. However, I did have to get up extremely early to take reference photographs of them before they descended from their normal perch in the oak tree in order to see what they looked like from below. The reason for this is a matter of perspective. The eye-level of the observer would naturally be lower than the birds, so to make them look realistic, I needed to view them from a similar angle.

Small Projects

The important thing about doing something like this bird, or the tabby cat featured on page 70, is that the wit of the joke will only be successful if you apply everything else in the book. By this I mean that considering the eye-level, doing the drawing well and matching colors to achieve realism will all contribute to the enjoyment of the onlooker. Keep the outline clean and well-defined.

A simple trompe l'oeil like this can have just as much impact in your house as a full-scale project but will only take a fraction of the time.

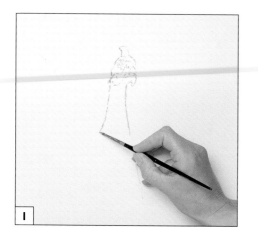 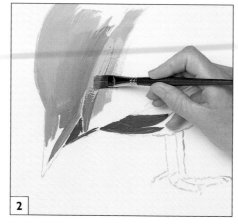 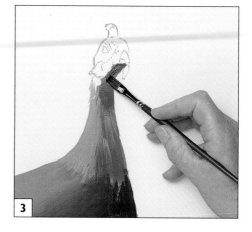

1 I took my outline from photographs of the guinea fowl. To enlarge the outline to the correct size, I squared it up (see page 57) onto a large piece of tracing paper. Draw with a soft pencil on the reverse side of the paper, then hold the paper against the wall and go over the outline again with a harder pencil on the right side to make a faint outline. Sketch in the outline using dilute Payne's grey and white and a fine pointed brush.

2 Block in the solid bird shape with the 1 cm (½ in) flat brush, using Payne's grey, white, raw umber and burnt sienna with more Payne's grey in the shadowy areas. Continue with the same four colors, working deeper into the shadow areas to describe the shape of the bird. Bear in mind the direction of the light.

3 Add a little quinacridone crimson, and ultramarine to the shadow side of the neck using a 1 cm (½ in) flat brush. At this stage, the painting is quite sketchy. It is important to wait for each application of paint to dry before beginning the next color, otherwise it will slide off the wall when you overpaint.

4 Rough in the red parts of the head with cadmium red using a small pointed brush. Add the eye, nostril, horn and legs, using burnt sienna, cadmium red and cadmium yellow. Also put in the shadows and folds of the red parts with crimson, burnt sienna and Payne's grey. The head is pure white and should stand out against the off white background.

5 Add highlights and shadows to the chest area using a 1 cm (½ in) flat brush, working more into the shadows and always softening between highlight and shadow as you work over the previous coat. It helps to imagine the bird without its spots.

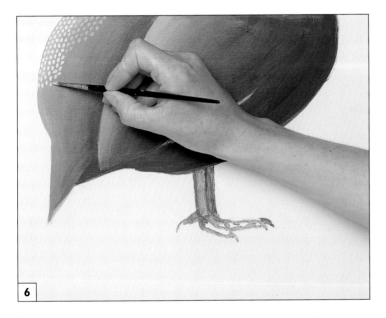

6 Now you are ready to do the spots. Look closely at your reference or first sketch the pattern of the spots on paper to look at. Don't worry too much about accuracy – no one really counts spots on guinea fowl! Using a fine pointed brush, paint patches of spots and then fill in the gaps. Make the spot shape elliptical near the edges to add to the illusion of roundness. Use white in the sunlit areas, and grey (by adding Payne's grey) in the shadows in varying amounts depending on the darkness.

7 Using a 2 cm (¾ in) flat brush and the background color, tidy up the edges of the guinea fowl for a neat finish.

Cattle Murals

These paintings were commissioned by David Bennett who wanted to commit his favorite cow and bull to posterity. The bull is led by his herdsman, dressed in nineteenth-century clothing which he felt suitable for the occasion.

The bull and cow were long since deceased, but David had some pictures of them from which I could establish their markings. I painted the cow standing in front of Blair Castle in Perthshire as that was where she had gone to live when David had sold her. For reference I used a photo of the castle.

PAINTS

Cadmium red
Yellow ochre
Cadmium yellow
Permanent light
  green
Cobalt blue
Payne's grey
Raw umber
White

EQUIPMENT

5 mm (¼ in) flat
  brush
1 cm (½ in) flat
  brush
Fine pointed brush

Painting Trees

The tree in this painting is a rather stylised elm. It was painted on a tinted surface (see page 55). The redness helps foliage look more lively. First work out what sort of tree you want in your painting as every tree is different. The best way to learn about tree colors is to take the color index (see page 50) outside and look at trees, trying to match selected patches of color to a particular card. This will teach you that tree greens, like grass greens, are amazingly red, and you will need to add surprising amounts of cadmium red to each color. To paint a tree like this you need seven colors: four greens, and three trunk colors, i.e. a sort of greeny-grey in three tones.

If you are working on a big scale, it may help to paint the leaves with a sponge roller cut into leaf patterns with a craft knife. You could also make a leaf stencil. Leaves on a tree tell you what sort of tree it is, and all the leaves are exactly the same size and shape, but viewed from slightly different angles, so that a stencil with, say, five leaves at different angles to the viewpoint could be used to paint huge areas of foliage. This tree, however, is small and fairly simple.

The rough edges of the painting are intentional, as if the new paint has been scraped off to reveal these paintings underneath.

1 First, block in the approximate shape of the foliage with the second darkest green, using a 1 cm (½ in) flat brush. This actually shows the reverse side of the tree, where the leaves face outwards – you are looking at the backs of these leaves.

2 Using a mixture of raw umber and Payne's grey and a fine pointed brush, sketch in the skeleton of the tree. Remember that a tree must be well balanced otherwise it will fall over! This is best learnt by observation.

3 Now you have the inside and far side of the tree. Visualize some branches coming towards you and some going away from you. Using the pointed brush, pick out some of the topsides of the branches (remembering the direction of the light source) in a lighter color, e.g. raw umber, Payne's grey, white and a little yellow ochre.

4 Instead of trying to picture all the individual leaves and twigs on the tree, simplify the leaves into clumps of foliage and imagine them pointing towards you and sideways. Paint them using a 1 cm (½ in) brush and the lightest green for the topsides, the middle shade for the bulk of the clump, and the darkest shade for the shadowy undersides.

5 Carry on painting in this way, building up convincing clumps of foliage. I used a 5 mm (¼ in) flat brush and a fine sable for the small branches. Don't be afraid to rework the branches in gaps between the leaves.

6 Finally, bring the sky and background colors in to outline the tree, and using a 5 mm (¼ in) brush, puncture the green canopy with dots of the sky colors to make it all look less solid.

En Grisaille

En Grisaille implies that little or no color has been used in the painting, giving it a monochromatic effect. This project wouldn't appeal to those with insufficient patience as the technique I used here to produce this rather ghostly effect is time-consuming but very satisfying when finished. My clients had enormous fun choosing the nine characters featured on the walls and the room ended up being quite extraordinary.

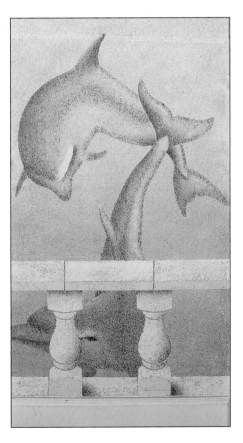

En Grisaille Details

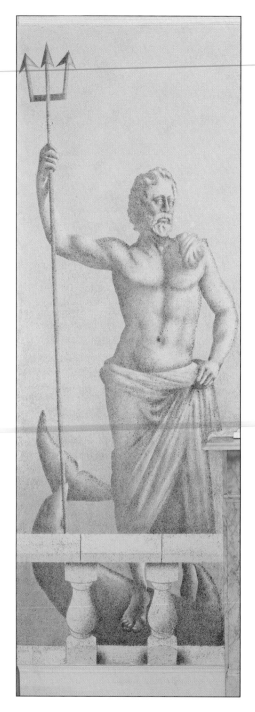

The walls of this room were very uneven, so to disguise this I used a highly textured background and a splattered effect for the painting. The balustrade was the first element of the work, concealing a bump which circled the entire room where a dado rail had been removed. Once the balustrade existed there seemed to be an amazing space outside it, as though the actual surface of the walls had disappeared. This was when the mythological figures came into being, one by one, until there were nine in total, including Pegasus, the winged horse; Neptune, god of the sea; and Athena, goddess of war, wisdom and the arts and crafts.

All the figures are mythological, except for the man climbing over the trompe l'oeil balustrade, who appears to be intruding into this fantasy. He was the first to be painted and was dressed in clothes copied from late-eighteenth century Piranesi prints. Climbing into the room, his eyes are fixed on his lover who is dressed as Athena. Perhaps they are both aware of the other fantastic figures. She holds up a golden bridle, inviting him to jump on to the back of Pegasus. The other seven figures gaze at this from their ghostly world outside the balustrade. Only the man and woman are 'real' which is why they are painted in color.

PAINTS

White
Burnt umber
Cerulean blue
Cobalt blue
Jenkins green
Burnt sienna

EQUIPMENT

2 old lambswool
  rollers with a
  long shaggy pile
Large piece of old
  board
Toothbrush
2 natural sponges,
  one fist-sized
  and one smaller
2B pencil
Flat 1 cm (½ in)
  brush
Low-tack masking
  tape, 2.5 cm
  (1 in) wide
Small pointed
  brush

Pegasus

For this background I used three greys
– light, medium and dark – mixed
using varying amounts of white, burnt
umber and cerulean blue. These
colors also formed the basis for all the
underpainting of the figures, the
details of which were done with paint
first painted on with a brush, then
enhanced by flicking on extra paint
with a toothbrush.

    The two flicked colors were blue
(made with cobalt blue, Jenkins green,
a drop of burnt umber and a little
white) and a dilution of burnt sienna.

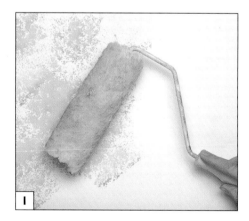

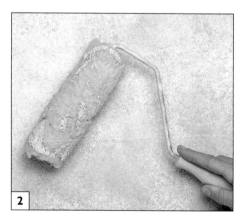

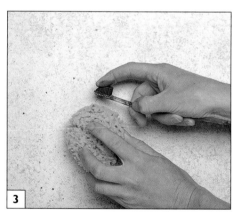

1 Start by boldly attacking the wall with a
lambswool roller and the darkest grey paint.
Ideally use an old one because the pile gives a
more broken surface. Rather than immersing
the roller into deep puddles of paint, paint a
square of the color you are using onto a
board so that the pile of the roller picks up
only a small amount of paint, making the
surface even rougher.

2 Repeat this step, using all three shades of
grey. In this mural I started with a dark grey and
got lighter as I progressed. I also made the top
of the walls much lighter than the bottom, so
that the balustrade would really stand out.
(The balustrade was done using a stencil –
for instructions see page 66.)

3 Using an old toothbrush, flick just a little of
the blue onto the background and dab it with
the fist-sized sponge, using a slightly twisting
motion, to give just a hint of the blue all over.

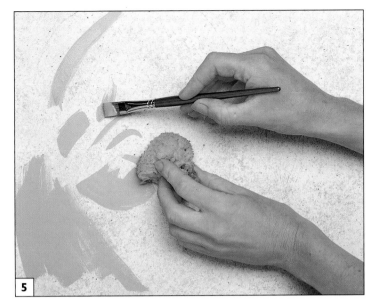

4 Next comes the outline. Using a 2B pencil, sketch in the horse, making a really clean, accurate edge. (This outline was 'borrowed' from Stubbs' *Whistlejacket* and 'adapted' to become Pegasus!) For confidence, use an overhead projector to project your drawing on to the wall or square up (see page 57).

5 Use the darkest of the three shades of grey to sketch in the shadowy areas, using a flat 1 cm (½ in) brush and softening the edges with the smaller natural sponge as you go.

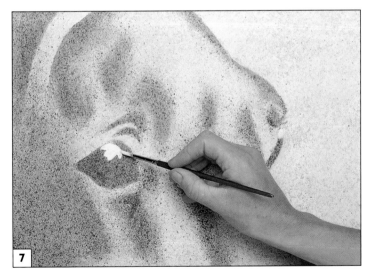

6 Using short lengths of the low-tack masking tape, mask off outside each shadow and carefully flick alternate blue and burnt sienna into the shadow using a toothbrush. Remove tape as you finish one area and retape another area. You can tape several areas at once to save refuelling the toothbrush too often. I also find it economical to reuse the tape.

7 Use a small pointed brush and the lightest grey to emphasize any areas you wish to, and use an almost white shade of grey to highlight any special areas such as the eye.

Changing Room

The funny thing about the keys and the banknote in this trompe l'oeil is that they are what people notice. The curtains which 'dress' the arch through to the swimming pool, and all the fictitious clothing hanging on the pegs to the right, even the lady's bottom sticking out from behind the billowing curtain often escape the attention of the onlooker, but never the money and the keys!

My brief was to decorate the long wall next to the indoor pool at the Nare Hotel in Cornwall. There was no point trying to surpass the stunning views – the scenery is simply too beautiful to compete with. So I did the opposite. I painted something very down-to-earth and mundane, with a touch of 'tongue in cheek'.

Fabric Effects

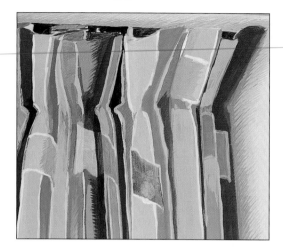

Above Making fabric look as though it is scrunched up can be done (in this case) by making the stripes on the material much narrower where the curtain tape would be, and also changing to 'shadow' colors in the 'cracks'.

Right Humor is an important factor in trompe l'oeil. Did she know that her bottom was sticking out? In order to learn how to paint any part of the human anatomy, find out about local life painting classes. As usual, my best advice is that observation can solve all the problems you may think you have! All the information you need is right in front of you if you choose to look!

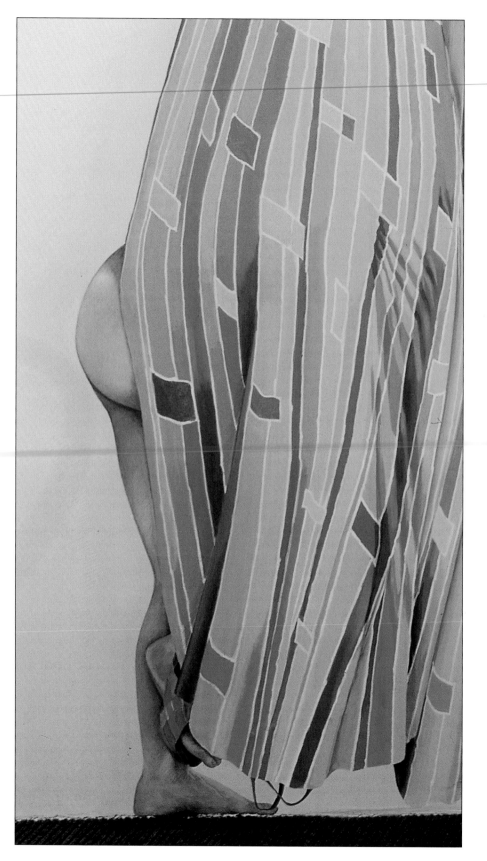

The whole room was repainted at my request, so that I would not have to work on a white background. White walls are an absolute killer for trompe l'oeil effects, as there is no 'room' for painting highlights. You need to save white for special occasions to gain the maximum impact of its brightness. The background color that I often use in a situation like this where the client would prefer the room to look white is 0705Y10R. This color is a very subtle pale creamy-greeny-grey. It's much nicer than white anyway!

These clothes were all painted from life. To help me to look carefully at the folds of the fabric, I hung and draped the clothes around me, making sure the light was always on the left so that they appeared to be lit by light from the window of the pool. The idea was that the swimmers had left their clothes on the pegs, revealing something of their characters!

Burnt sienna
Cadmium yellow
Cadmium red
Payne's grey
White
Raw umber
Burnt umber

EQUIPMENT

Large domed
    continental
    brush
Open grain natural
    sponge
Toothbrush
Small radiator
    roller
Chalk
I cm (½ in) flat
    brush

Creating Stonework

The bunch of keys and the money lying on this 'granite' stone bench were an afterthought, and yet they attract more attention than the rest of the painting! The step-by-step photographs on these pages show how I painted the stone to look realistic but the most important piece of advice I can give if you are intending to paint some 'stone' is to look at some! When trying to show the texture and subtle colors of stone you can make life so much easier for yourself by closely examining a lump of stone of the type you wish to describe. The nature of every rock formation is so different – I keep lots of different pieces of rock in my studio for reference.

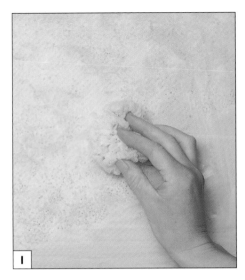

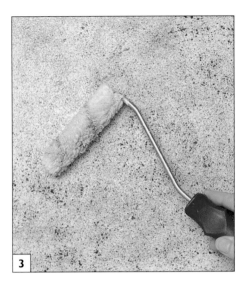

1 Paint over the entire area with a large domed continental brush, using a very diluted mixture of burnt sienna, cadmium yellow and red, and quickly sponge vigorously with an open grain natural sponge.

2 Using a toothbrush, flick Payne's grey all over the area to give more depth to the texture.

3 Add a pale grey (mixed from white, burnt sienna and Payne's grey) with a small radiator roller, rolling it haphazardly all over.

4 Wash over with Payne's grey and raw umber diluted with water, and sponge again. Repeat as many times as you like until the surface looks really gritty.

5 When you are happy with the grittiness, sketch the keys and banknote with chalk and, using a I cm (½ in) flat brush, build up a shadow around it with a wash of raw umber and Payne's grey. As with the clothes, the keys and banknote are best observed from life, and painted as you would a still life with the objects in front of you for reference.

The Monk

My research for this painting took me to Buckland Abbey where the monks helped me to crystallize my thoughts. I photographed a model of the abbey and its surrounding buildings to help the composition of the 'outside'. The background landscape was sheer fantasy, based on a mixture of inspiration from the front cover of a magazine and our local Camel Estuary, looking out towards Padstow. I painted this monk on a panel for a trompe l'oeil exhibition in London, but I had in mind a particular spot in a wonderful priory in Somerset, which was being renovated. He is a Cistercian monk, gazing down into the cloister from high above, lost in thought, and oblivious to the dove, who has not noticed the cat, who has not noticed the mouse (see full picture overleaf).

If you tip the picture plane forwards (as if tipping a sheet of glass) in order to look down (see page 19), the horizon naturally rises which is why the distant hills are higher than the normal 1.5 m (5 ft) eye level. I used all sorts of tricks to make the outside much lighter and brighter than the gloomy interior where he stands. The whole painting started with a vigorous sponging and washing of warm diluted colors, mixtures of cadmium red, burnt sienna, yellow ochre and cadmium yellow with a good bit of flicking with toothbrushes and dabbing with dishcloths. By overpainting the 'interior' bits with washes of Payne's grey and raw umber, I was quickly able to establish the feeling of being in a gloomy place looking out into the bright daylight.

PAINTS

Payne's grey
White
Raw umber
Yellow ochre
Matt acrylic
   medium

EQUIPMENT

1 cm (½ in) flat
   brush
Fine pointed brush
2.5 cm (1 in) flat
   brush

Monk's Sleeve

In this area of the trompe l'oeil I
wanted to make the cloth of the
monk's habit look colorless and
gloomy, so I draped some similar
lengths of fabric to see how colors
were affected as they lost light in the
depths of the folds. Glazing over, as
expained in step 5, helped to keep the
monk in his gloom.

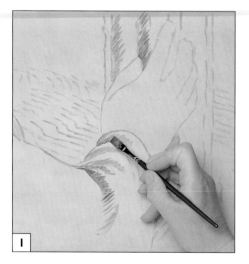

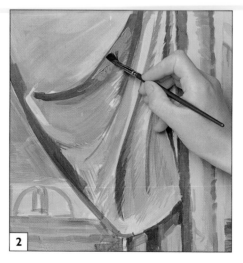

1 Using the 1 cm (½ in) brush, sketch with
diluted Payne's grey and white onto the warm
background and, even at this early stage, show
the shadows by sketching with the brush. This
helps you to work out the folds.

2 Block in the main areas very roughly,
strengthening and extending the depth of the
shadows with a mixture of raw umber and
Payne's grey. The main thing at this stage is to
build up all areas of the painting loosely before
starting to bring it together in any detail.

3 The lighter tones of the cloth can be shown
in loose sweeping brush strokes, using the 1 cm
(½ in) brush and adding white and yellow ochre
to the mixture of Payne's grey and raw umber.
Remember to balance the darkness inside the
building with the contrasting light outside
(i.e. keep the figure darker than the landscape
outside). Soften the folds of the cloth by cross-
hatching with color as you would with a pencil.

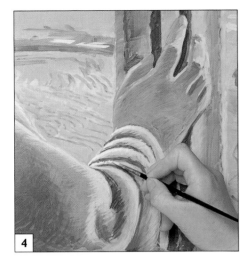

4 Using the same colors, keep building light and shade in and out of the folds of the fabric, softening all the time by cross-hatching. Some of the folds may need a fine brush. It really helps to have suitable fabric hanging close to you to look at, so that you know what it is you are trying to achieve. You can even use the color index (see page 50) to find colors in the folds of the fabric which will help so much to describe the texture.

5 To strengthen the darkness of the monk's habit use a dark glaze made with raw umber, Payne's grey, and matt acrylic medium, applied with the 2.5 cm (1 in) brush. Do this several times as it adds to the gloom, thereby exaggerating the brightness outside.

A Cornish Window

All murals have a reason, and here is the reason for this one! I don't need to have rural views painted inside my Cornish farmhouse as all the views from the windows are wonderful anyway. But for several years now we have had terrible weather during the summer, and the days when we can visit our favorite beach on the north coast are few and far between.

This year there was suddenly such a day. A crystal-clear, beautiful, shining day. The first glimpse of this beach as you clambered down the cliff path was so breathtaking that I felt moved to have this view out of a trompe l'oeil window behind the kitchen sink where my spirits most often need lifting. I had taken my camera and the color index with me and spent time considering the best view. I decided to balance the cliffs on the left by putting the open window on the other side.

Window Details

The flowers were a spontaneous addition. When I picked them, I had no idea that they would be so powerful. I just love wild flowers, and had no reservations about looking at them from the kitchen sink position, or from anywhere else in the room.

It is my belief that there is a kind of inner spiritual peace to be found during the painting of flowers from life. Avoid photographic reference wherever possible and look at the real thing. I find myself becoming inwardly calm and almost completely absorbed in the wonderful intricacies of petal colors and formations and thus entering a state of quiet, rather like the peace of a church or museum. There is something so amazing about the way a flower is put together that you can't help but be respectful and feel rather humble. The problem is to pack in enough observation and painting time before the flower fades in front of you.

Try to set aside enough time for this rather than do the painting over an extended period. The flowers will be long gone, but your impression of them will remain fresh forever. These flowers were all picked from the hedgerow and I had to replace some of them because as the painting progressed as I couldn't work fast enough to capture the quality I was looking for.

There are full instructions for painting the sea and waves in The White Horses project on pages 110-111.

PAINTS

Full palette of
colors (see
page 51)

EQUIPMENT

Chalk line
Chalk
Fine pointed brush
Sword-line brush
for very fine
lines

The Flowers

This wall had one or two cracks and, having removed paintings from the wall and extracted the picture hooks, I needed to do some filling. I lightly sanded the whole wall and wiped it with a damp cloth before starting. I primed the area involved in the actual painting of the window with two coats of gesso, sanded between coats.

I used the color index (see page 50) to decipher colors, looking carefully at the sky, sea and sand, and making pencil notes on the color index. I had a lot of fun painting the sea, trying to make it transparent. The success of this depends on observation and using the right colors.

To paint the flowers, first draw in chalk on the background which may already be well advanced. Don't worry about finishing it before starting the flowers. It is almost impossible to paint so perfectly that you don't mark the bits you have already painted. It is better to try and amalgamate the two as you go, even if it means carefully painting around stalks and so on.

I used the projection method (see page 26) to establish the vanishing point for the top, bottom and glazing bars of the imaginary window.

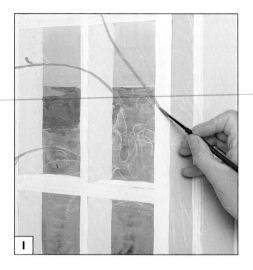

1 After sketching in chalk and using the chalk line for the vertical lines, use the fine pointed brush to start sketching in the stems in a shade of mid-green, made with permanent green light, yellow ochre, white and cadmium red. (Use plenty of red in greens used for painting foliage.) I use a full palette of colors for painting complicated subjects like this.

5 Sketch the shapes of the purple irises roughly before building the detail.

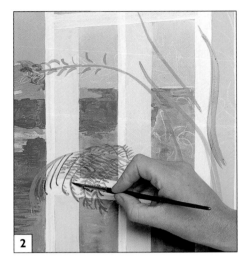

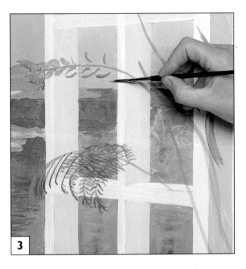

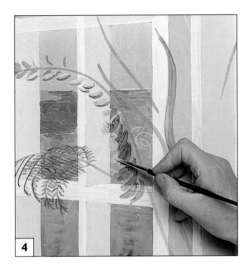

2 Continue adding additional detail to the shapes of the leaves and the ferns using the fine pointed brush.

3 Start to block in flowers and foliage, observing the flowers very, very closely to see how the light affects the colors you are looking at. Here the deep pink undersides of the foxgloves are being added.

4 Continue to work, treating the painting as a still life. Here, paler pink foxglove petals are being painted. You have to be quick before the flowers droop. When they start to fade, pick new ones rather than let the droopy, dying ones influence your painting.

6 Once you have the main shapes in position you can begin adding detail to the flowers using the sword-line brush.

7 I painted the buttercups white before painting them yellow. With transparent bright colors (yellow, red and green), you can achieve more brightness by doing it this way. The buttercups look more three-dimensional if you shadow the inside of the petals with their backs to the light.

8 Add the finishing touches to the flowers, such as the dark spots on the pale insides of the foxglove petals.

The White Horses

I was amazed when a major beer company ran an advertising campaign just like this mural, and would have been fascinated to meet the designer who must have had identical thoughts on the subject, i.e. turning the crests of breaking waves into white horses leaping wildly from the water.

I adapted a Roman mosaic to form the basis of my design, and Neptune became a muscular surfer as this area of Cornwall is so famous for its surfers. The trompe l'oeil illusion was created by using a series of columns and arches along the length of the walls. Fragments of scattered masonry along the base of the wall help to suggest a collapsing ruin being reclaimed by the sea (not at all the case here at the Watergate Bay Hotel which has the most incredible views of the sea).

PAINTS

White
Payne's grey
Yellow ochre
Burnt sienna
Raw umber
(For sky colors,
   see page 112)

EQUIPMENT

Chalk line
Radiator roller
Car-washing
   sponge
Fine sable brush

Sandstone Columns

When designing this trompe l'oeil I used a height of 1.5 m (5 ft) from the floor as my eye-level. This height therefore became the level for the horizon of the sea.

When you draw columns, start by imagining that they are square, not circular (see page 29). Using a vanishing point on the eye-level, you can draw the sides of the square to the vanishing point and then use the diagonals of the square base and top to draw a convincing circle in the correct perspective. Columns are narrower at the top and widen out roughly two-thirds of the way down. From there downwards, they are straight and true verticals.

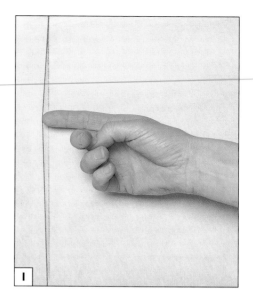

1 Mark out the columns using a chalk line, adding 1 cm (½ in) to the width two-thirds of the way down.

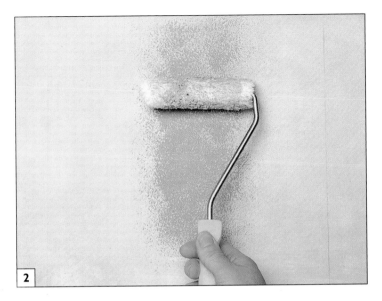

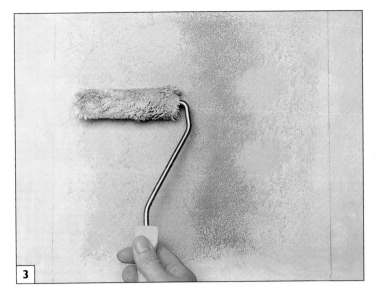

2 I used a radiator roller and three different sandstone colors – light, medium and dark, mixed as follows:

Light color: white, Payne's grey, yellow ochre and burnt sienna
Medium color: white, yellow ochre and burnt sienna
Dark color: white, raw umber and yellow ochre
Paint the middle of the column with the medium color.

3 The darkest bit is inside and off-centre away from the strongest implied light source (i.e. from the left). Carry on using the three colors to form the cylinder using your imagination to feel the light (here, coming from the left, so the lightest color appears on the left).

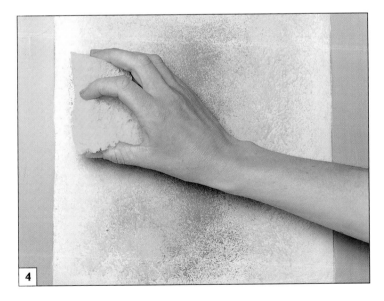

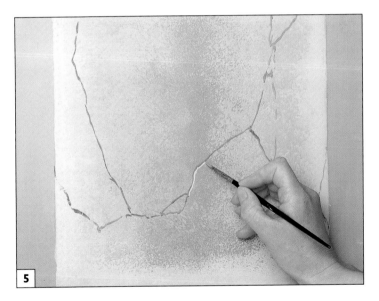

4 Painting the background in as soon as possible gives you something to relate to and make sure it's working. You can dab on the edge colors with a square-edged car washing sponge (or similar). Develop the texture all over by repeatedly overpainting with sponges and rollers, using all three colors.

5 Finally, use a fine sable brush to add a few cracks, with a mixture of raw umber and Payne's grey. It doesn't really matter how you do this, but remember to try and make them curve around the column. Highlighting the lower edge of the crack with a light color gives it more depth.

PAINTS

White
Payne's grey
Burnt sienna
Yellow ochre

EQUIPMENT

2.5 cm (1 in) flat
brush
Soft dishcloth

Horse's Head

I have always loved to imagine that the foaming tops of waves are wild white horses rearing out of the water, tossing their wild manes. I was delighted when the owners of the Watergate Bay Hotel commissioned this painting. Searching through some magazines, I found some amazing, heavyweight French working horses. I slimmed them down a bit, thinking they might sink! I did a lot of sketches, then transferred my drawing to acetate to project an outline on the wall.

1 Having sorted out the drawing problems on paper, then projected the image on to the wall, it's easy to start painting with confidence because you know where you are going! Working on a colored background (in this case a mushroom color) helps to establish light and shadow much quicker than if you started on a white background.

2 Working with large flat brushes, rough in light and shadow right from the beginning of the painting, taking great care not to get too light or too dark as you need to save those values right till the end. (In this case the foam was the only pure white used.)

3 Use a damp folded pad of dishcloth (of the supermarket floorcloth kind) to blend and soften the acrylics as you paint.

PAINTS

Ultramarine blue
Raw umber
White
Quinacridone
   crimson
Pthalo green
Dioxazine purple
Cadmium yellow
Cadmium red
Payne's grey

EQUIPMENT

Chalk line
Low-tack masking
   tape
8 mm (⅜ in) flat
   brush
1 cm (½ in) brush
Large domed
   continental
   brush
Fine pointed brush
Dishcloth

Sea and Waves

First, look at the sea! If you are not lucky enough to have some nearby, look carefully at some reference material. Identify some colors using the color index (see page 50). To do this, hold the index cards up at arms length making sure that they are in a good, even light. By shutting one eye, and looking from the sea to the color card nearest to the same color, you should, with practice, be able to select, say, five important colors. Mix these using the paints suggested.

The sea moves in triangular ridges of different sizes. When the wind is blowing hard, the surface of the water becomes very broken and the colors difficult to decipher. The easiest way to look

closely at the way the colors work is when there has been a storm a long way away, but the local wind is negligible, or off-shore, so that the surface is quite smooth and unruffled, but the waves big enough to show the different planes and angles.

If you imagine that the blocks are long triangles heading towards you, try noticing that the back of the triangle is reflecting the sky and through the front of the triangle you can see down into the water which is usually green, the shade depending upon the depth and the type of shore or ocean bottom underneath. The deeper the water, the darker the color. As the block thins towards the top, before breaking over itself, the color of the green is lighter, meaning it is more transparent.

By using blues and greys which reflect the sky and different greens which describe the depths, you can paint the waves convincingly. Always keep the colors darker than you would imagine, so that the foam can gleam. This is not possible to achieve if all your colors are too light and bright.

It's difficult to blend one color smoothly into another when using acrylics. Like painting sky (see page 112), you might like to use a damp dishcloth to blend the paint. Don't worry if you have to do it several times to achieve the desired effect – I always do!

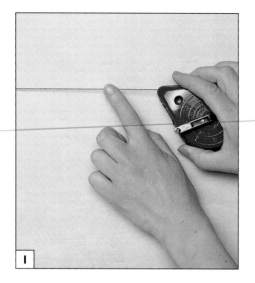

1 Mark in the horizon at 1.5 m (5 ft) with the chalk line. Here the horizon was almost 20 m (22 yards) long so I had to make lots of marks at the horizon level with an assistant holding the other end of the string. If you haven't got help, stick one end of the string to the wall with low-tack tape. Paint in the sky (see page 112).

2 Begin painting the sea with the 8 mm (⅜ in) brush and a dark blue-grey horizon color. This could be a mixture of ultramarine blue, raw umber, white, a little quinacridone crimson and a touch of pthalo green.

3 Use a lighter blue to paint the waves just below the horizon. For interest, interrupt the blue with some green waves. You can help the illusion tremendously by making the waves tiny near the horizon.

4 Paint the waves bigger towards the foreground, making long sweeping strokes with the 1 cm (½ in) flat brush, using a lighter blue-grey, interrupted with dark greeny blues.

5 Start to build the waves towards the foreground. It doesn't matter if there are gaps. Keep looking at the real sea or at your reference pictures. It is so important to have a feel for the movement of the waves in order to avoid becoming too static. You might find painting waves a bit like spotting faces in flames. It is a sort of abstract painting but the character of each wave develops as you go on, and once you have your basic shape you can build on it. Right in the foreground you will need to use a large domed continental brush to get the coverage.

6

7

6 With a small brush you can paint in little white horses in the distance. The smaller you paint them, the greater the distance will appear to be. Use a mixture of white and Payne's grey for this, and be very careful not to make them too white as you need to save white for the foreground foam for the greatest impact.

7 Keep building up shapes and colors, trying to imagine these triangular blocks of water rolling towards you. When a wave breaks, all sorts of complicated things happen – the painting of a single wave could occupy a whole book on its own! Here we must simplify. The wave becomes more transparent – a lighter green at the top, before toppling over and falling down the front of the triangle.

8

9

8 When this happens use white to paint the foam, with a mixture of white and Payne's grey where the foam shadows itself to make it less flat.

9 The breaking wave also makes a reflection on the surface between the triangles. Try spotting this for real. I used a golden green made with cadmium yellow, cadmium red and some of my brightest wave color to paint this reflection. There are two other odd reflections that I put into this mural, I put flecks of the base color (mushroom) in horizontal rows in the concave part of the breaking wave. This bright gold speckle of color helps to make it look wet. There is also a horizontal ultraviolet line lower in the curve of the wave. The ultraviolet is just a little removed from the darkest green, so by adding a touch of dioxazine purple, ultramarine blue and white to that, you should find another reflection developing.

PAINTS

Ultramarine blue
Cobalt blue
White
Pthalo green
Burnt sienna
Yellow ochre
Cadmium yellow
Cadmium red
Payne's grey
Raw umber
Dioxazine purple
Quinacridone
    crimson

EQUIPMENT

Domed continental
    brush
Damp dishcloth
    (not the
    colored kind)
2.5 cm (1 in) flat
    wash brush
Squirrel or similar
    soft brush
Film canisters or
    jam jars for
    small projects;
    empty paint
    cans for larger
    skies

Sky and Clouds

The amazing thing about skies is how dark and different in color they are from the plain blue and white mixture we might have assumed! Using the color index to identify colors (see page 50) by either looking at real sky or a good photo will teach you a lot. Try to isolate three or four patches of color, starting just above the horizon and then allowing your eye to move up until you are looking at the 'top' of the sky. In each level, find a matching color on the index.

Starting with the nearest blue (I often use either cobalt or ultramarine), try to mix an identical color. First you will need to add white, but this mixture alone will be far too bright. I usually make three or four shades to paint a sky, storing each color in an airtight container as several applications may be needed and acrylics tend to change color slightly as they dry which makes matching a previously applied color difficult. To the blue and white mixture I added small quantities of pthalo green, burnt sienna, dioxazine purple and Payne's grey for the 'upper' colors. Nearer the bottom, where the haze is thicker and the sky appears greyer, add a dash of raw umber, quinacridone crimson and cadmium red plus more white.

Try doing this for yourself, matching the colors you have picked out exactly. It is this choice of color which is so important in creating illusions like the Tuscan View (see page 62) or A Cornish Window (see page 98). Quite often the sky will appear to the onlooker as super-bright, when actually it's the relationship between the sky color and the rest of the painting which gives it the depth.

Painting clouds is rather like painting waves (see page 109) – it's controlled abstraction. Look at clouds before you start and try to observe how they are made and how they move. Use colors matched to either reality or to a good photograph with the color index. Clouds are not white nor are they grey, made with black and white! They are subtle shades of browns, and complex greys made with blues, browns and purples.

1 Prepare the background as on page 55, using washes of warm colors such as mixtures of cadmium red, burnt sienna, yellow ochre and cadmium yellow. Slosh the paint on boldly with a large domed continental brush. It will help you to 'break in' the surface.

2 Dab at the surface with a damp dishcloth to even out the texture. Repeat these two steps until you feel the surface has a good ground color to work on.

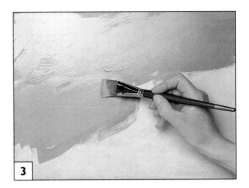

3 Mix your colors. Use a wide flat brush to paint horizontal strips, working two colors into each other with the brush (you may prefer to use a couple of brushes here, so that one stays in one color and another in your next color). Don't paint too much at one go, as the paint will dry too quickly for you to smooth it out.

4 Soften the edges between colors immediately with a damp dishcloth. If you don't get perfection first time, don't worry. Just wait for the paint to dry completely and go again, working systematically in horizontal stripes from top to bottom and back up again. The quality of the sky will improve each time, and the warm underpainting will give it an extra ingredient.

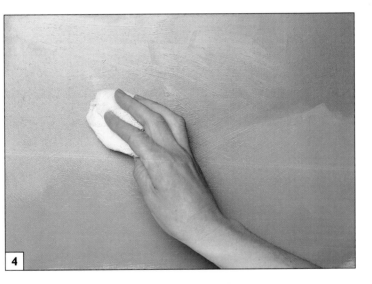

5 These clouds were painted using a mixture of white, raw umber, Payne's grey and dioxazine purple. I used a soft squirrel brush for a rather haphazard effect. On a large scale use a domed continental brush. Avoid overworking the shape.

6 Soften the edges of the cloud immediately with a clean damp dishcloth.

7 Bearing in mind the light source (in other words the position of the sun), use the squirrel brush to squiggle in some highlights using a carefully chosen color. I used one made with white, raw umber, ultramarine and burnt sienna.

8 Soften the highlights with the damp dishcloth, and continue until you are happy with the effect.

Painted Furniture

Trompe l'oeil can so easily be used on furniture to add both interest and, as usual, humor to an otherwise rather dull household object.

This is a decorative idea that might liven up any plain furniture. I wanted to make the wood really glow like mahogany. For the draped silk cloth I found a wonderful picture by Ingrès called *La Grande Odalisque,* which inspired this painting. It would have been acceptable, I think, to have just done the firescreen as if it was carved mahogany, but I liked the idea of the casually draped piece of silk damask. It begged the question who had left it there and why. An element of mystery always adds to trompe l'oeil!

PAINTS

Cadmium red
Burnt umber
Raw umber
Dioxazine purple
Ultramarine blue
Jenkins green
White
Payne's grey
Light violet
Yellow ochre
Cadmium yellow
Matt acrylic glaze
    (satin finish)

EQUIPMENT

Large hogs' bristle
    domed
    continental
    brush
Tracing paper
2B and 6B pencils
Low-tack masking
    tape
8 mm (³⁄₈ in) flat
    brush
Fine pointed brush

The Firescreen

Fireplaces can look very dingy in the summer when the fire's not lit, so why not add something a little exotic to a simple firescreen which can be purchased unpainted. I found a picture in a magazine of a Rococo carved mahogany headboard which gave me the idea for the pattern at the top. I placed a polished mahogany chest near me in the studio so that I could observe what happened to its color both in the light and in shadow. To see how the damask worked I hung up my daughter's silk blouse to help me understand the folds in the fabric.

I first primed the screen with black gesso, then used two shades of reddish-brown glaze to make the surface gleam like wood. I used the color index (see page 50) to match the color to real mahogany. The paint was mixed with matt acrylic glaze to dilute it and make it more transparent.

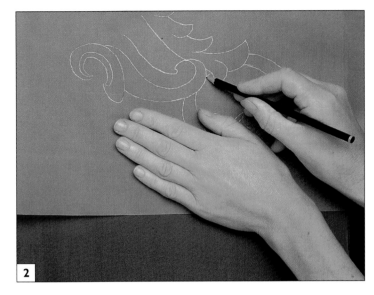

1 The glaze is made with cadmium red, burnt umber, raw umber and dioxazine purple, mixed with matt acrylic glaze. Paint it on with a large domed continental brush to leave streaks of the black showing through. Even after one coat, it's surprising how effective it is! Keep the brush strokes going in the same direction to create the woodgrain effect.

2 For the rococo carving at the top, I found a magazine photograph of a carved mahogany headboard. I adapted this to fit the firescreen and made a full-size drawing on tracing paper. You only need to do one side as the other side (which is partly covered by the cloth) is just a mirror image of the same tracing. Draw on the reverse side of the tracing paper with a very soft 6B pencil, then tape the tracing to the screen and draw the design on the right side with a harder pencil. This will leave a pencil line on the firescreen for guidance.

3 Roughly paint in the draped silk cloth using the 8 mm (⅜ in) flat brush. I made four shades of the color of the cloth using ultramarine blue, Jenkins green, white and dioxazine purple. Now using a mixture of burnt umber, Payne's grey and dioxazine purple, sketch outside your pencil pattern guidelines to show the shadows cast by the wood carving. Don't worry if it's a bit sketchy – you can elaborate as you go.

4 Painting something to look three-dimensional is an exercise in light and shade. It is vital to be aware of the light source all the time, so paint deeper into the shadows and exaggerate the highlights (I used light violet and white for the highlights). I kept using my first mahogany colors to make the prominent carved shapes stand out from the shadows, highlighting them with the fine pointed brush and varying shades of light violet and white as if the wood was tinged with daylight.

5 The draped damask could have been any fabric but I chose this extravagant fabric because I wanted something luxurious. It was painted entirely using four blue colors and the detailed embroidery shades of white, yellow ochre, Jenkins green, cadmium yellow and cadmium red, which mixed together in different amounts make wonderful gold colors. I used the fine pointed brush to make the cross-hatching effect.

Tiepolo Mural

Some murals are not true trompe l'oeil, but could still be described as an 'intent to deceive' as they mislead the onlooker into believing they are something which they are not. Sometimes a painting can be an admiration of the original artist's work, without any pretence that it's the real thing as the composition is different in order to fit available space. In this case, my client and I were fascinated by Tiepolo (1696-1770), so I painted several panels based on the work he did to decorate the Villa Valmarana. I had to alter the original compositions to fit the particular spaces available and in doing so I may have changed other things which were relevant to their original environment. It was a real pleasure painting these and simply discovering the various techniques Tiepolo used. You can learn so much from scrutinizing a famous artist's work.

PAINTS

Full palette
of colors
(see page 51)

EQUIPMENT

8 mm (⅜ in)
flat brush
Dishcloth
Toothbrush

Painting the Fan

In the original painting, the fan was not patterned, but my client and I felt that Tiepolo might not mind this small alteration as my painting benefitted from the extra interest. Adding detail to an area of the painting can draw attention to that spot and can be quick to paint. The fun was making these murals look as if they were painted 250 years ago by 'ageing' the look of the painting!

I imitated Tiepolo's style, texture and subject in all these paintings, altering the compositions to suit available spaces in the building. I wondered if he used dishcloths and toothbrushes!

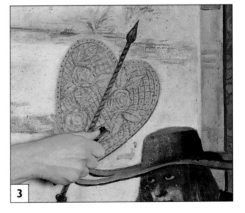

1 First, I sketched in the detail of the fan, working on one side at a time, then added white highlights.

2 Softening a complicated section of painting with an old dishcloth can add a vintage feel to the work in the simplest way. Fold the cloth into a pad and gently 'blot' the paint before it dries.

3 Using an old toothbrush, flick paint of a contrasting color on to the painting to further age it, and help the brush strokes to disappear.

The Arches

Although my client had originally asked me to paint a mural with a 'view' to the outside, I felt confident that an inner space would work better, especially as there were already French windows opening on to the garden from this lower ground floor room. Sometimes when a room already has a good view, I don't think there is any need to compete. It's better to use a bit of lateral thinking and approach the project from a different angle.

My first sketch showed how much 'view' I wanted to see through the opening within the nearest arch. This is extremely important because part of the perspective drawing process in this case is affected by the position of the viewpoint (see page 17) which you need to ascertain. All the perspective was done using the projection method and this is a very useful exercise in precision.

The composition of the painting was loosely based on a magazine photograph of the library at Longleat House. It had a second, deeper arch beyond the first, through which you could see an ascending staircase and a window in the distance. The floor was to be the main challenge, as I intended to make it look as though it was an extension of the existing floor, for which I needed to work out the vanishing points for the floor tiles which were set at an angle of 45 degrees to the picture plane (i.e. the wall).

Drawing the Plan

Step 1

First, set out the things you know. Do lots of rough sketches before you start working in scale to sort out your ideas. Use 'eyeballing' (estimates based on observation) and common sense to work out sizes of the imaginary arches.

When you are ready to work in scale set out a plan of the imaginary area as shown in blue, including the wall upon which it is painted, which is now known as the picture plane (shown in black). I have also included imaginary windows to help establish the light sources in the painting. (The arrows show the direction of the light coming into the fantasy rooms.)

Add the viewpoint below the plan (refer to page 23). The distance you stand from the picture plane affects the perspective, in particular the width of the view you will see through the 'opening'. If you stand too close, the view becomes much wider but angles become very distorted and it's better to imagine you are standing further away than you actually may be able to.

The area within the green lines shows how much you might see from this point of view. I have also shown the centre line in green.

Below the plan, draw an elevation, i.e. a view of the wall as we will actually see it, standing centrally. This means showing the ground line (bottom edge of the wall) and the height of it. The full-size opening can also be drawn on it as shown in black, and the outer stonework architrave which is not affected by perspective. Just sketch the curve at the top, remembering one side is a mirror image of the other. Add the eye-level, as shown in red. I usually use a height of 1.5 m (5 ft). Extend the eye-level, picture plane and ground line out to the sides as you need these lines for the projection.

Key	
Black lines:	*elements in real life, including edges of painted 'opening'*
Red lines:	*eye-level*
Blue lines:	*imaginary elements*
Green lines:	*important 'construction' lines*

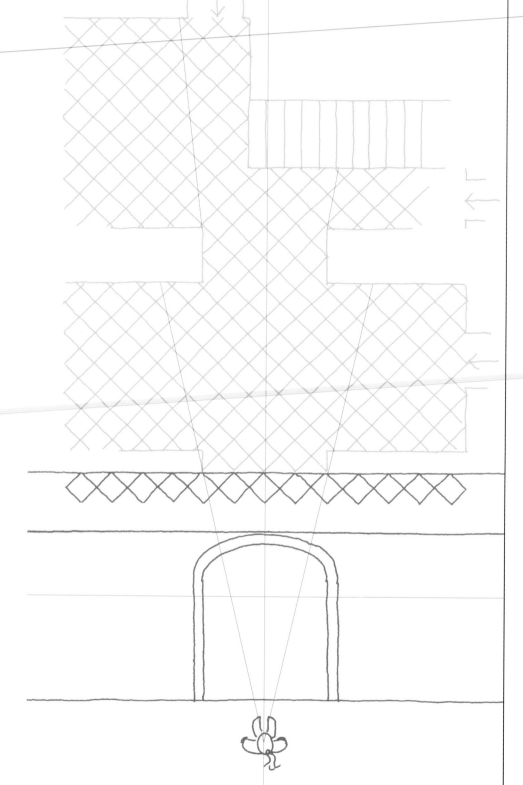

Step 2

Draw lines as shown in green connecting the viewpoint with important corners (i.e. the main points of architecture) in the plan. Where a line crosses the picture plane, drop it vertically down into the elevation to find the position of the vertical edge of that feature in perspective. This diagram only shows a few completed lines because the scale is so small, but when you do this, if you are using a scale of, for example, 1:10 or 1:20, the more lines, the better.

The floor tiles are shown on the plan both real and imaginary, taking special care to be accurate where they meet the wall itself (i.e. picture plane), and are shown at 45 degrees to the picture plane. Now draw lines parallel to the floor tiles in the plan from the viewpoint up to the picture plane as shown, one parallel to the left-hand edges and one parallel to the right hand edges. Where the lines meet the picture plane (on the left and right), drop vertically down to meet the eye level in the elevation. The points where they meet the eye-level are the vanishing points for the floor tiles in the perspective drawing.

For the arches, once you have the vertical lines, it helps to draw lines across the top imagining they are square at first. The reason is that drawing a line from the full height to the central vanishing point, crosses the 'back edge', the position of which you have now established, giving you the depth across the top as seen from this eye-level. When the eye- level as you look at an arch is near the top, the sides look fatter than the top.

Don't worry about refining the arch at this stage (page 128 shows how to draw an ellipse). All you need to know are the height and width which are the points the ellipse will touch.

Step 3

Now the three vanishing points can be used to complete the perspective drawing (elevation). The central one will establish the correct position for all lines which are parallel to the direction of view, e.g. the tops and bottoms of the arches.

The two points out to the side on the eye-level, which were arrived at in step 2, can be used to draw the floor tiles as shown, by connecting them to marks made where the tiles are full-size on the ground line. As you can see, in order to do the whole floor, you need to use imaginary marks further out to the sides along the ground line.

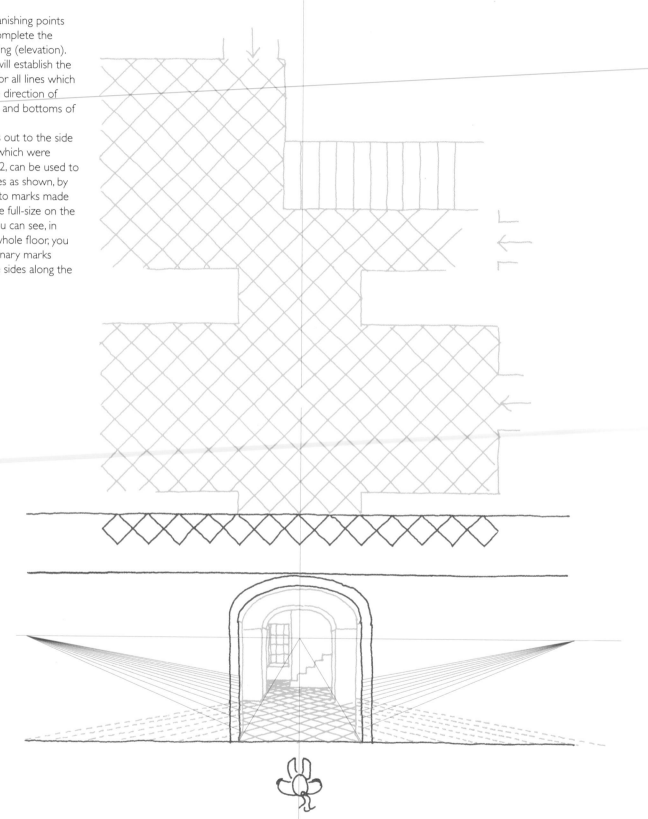

Step 4

Mark out the outline of the stairs to scale on the elevation. Note the angle at which the staircase rises. Draw lines from the intersections of treads and risers back to the central vanishing point.

Returning to your plan, find the position of the staircase in your painting by establishing important points as before. Start with the bottom step and once drawn, the rest will follow. The staircase in your 'view' will follow the same angle and each step will have the same dimensions as the first. Stairs rise at a constant angle, usually 35-40 degrees.

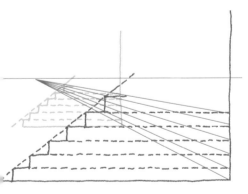

PAINTS	EQUIPMENT
Raw sienna	Masking tape
White	Scrap paper
Permanent light	Chalk line
violet	2.5 cm (1 in) flat
Raw umber	brush
Yellow ochre	Natural sponge
Payne's grey	8 mm (⅜ in) flat
Matt acrylic	brush
medium or a	Dishcloth
retarding medium	Fine pointed brush

The Floor

To get the information from the drawing on to the wall, either use reference points measured from the scale drawing, and convert back to full size, or trace the drawing on to acetate and project it, noting that the projector can distort architecture badly unless you are meticulous when positioning the projector to avoid tilting the image, the wall is flat and vertical and the floor is level! The first method is more reliable.

The perspective shown here will only be totally convincing from one central viewpoint. If you were to step sideways, of course, the perspective would no longer be completely accurate but I have found it very satisfying to achieve perfection from one spot anyway! Doing something like this could seem like a nightmare if you didn't have a few tricks up your sleeve! The idea of making a floor, tiled with square tiles set at 45 degrees to the picture plane (i.e. wall), appear to continue in your mural is best achieved on site as a certain amount of 'eyeballing' is called for, but a lot of the pain can be removed by technical preparation.

By glazing with thin paint (either mixed with water, or with matt acrylic medium or a retarding medium) you can achieve a chalky look which is especially good for natural stone floors.

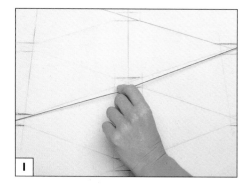

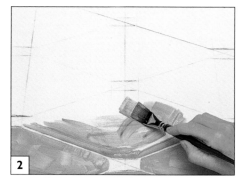

1 Guided either by measured reference points taken from your scale drawing or lines drawn with the overhead projector, use the chalk line to mark out the floor tiles. (An assistant is useful on a large mural.) If you make a mistake, wipe off the chalk and do it again. Accuracy is very important and can be checked by making sure that the intersections between the tiles form a line to the central vanishing point.

2 Using the 2.5 cm (1 in) flat brush, start to block in the tiles, mixing different variations of the same color for each tile. Leave a tiny gap either side of the chalk line, but keeping close to it and straight. I matched the color of the existing tiles using raw sienna, white, light violet (a surprisingly good stone color when mixed with yellow ochre or raw sienna), and adding some raw umber where I wanted the tiles to look darker, particularly in the shadowy places.

3 Carry on painting glazes using more light violet and white mixed with some yellow ochre for the lighter areas and more raw umber in the shadows.

4 Using a small natural sponge, soften brushmarks and blend the colors together. Leave gaps between the tiles.

5 If you are matching colors to an existing floor, keep standing back to compare colors (you can use the color index to help, see page 50). I needed to make the tiles more yellow to match. These tiles had a sort of ultraviolet bloom on them, made with light violet and white and used to exaggerate the implied light effect streaming in through imagined windows.

6 Block in the little squares with a mixture of raw umber, Payne's grey and white, using more white in the lighter bits, again as if they are touched by daylight. They are lighter than you would think. The sides of these go towards the central vanishing point.

7 Finally, remove the chalk lines with a damp cloth or sponge. Using a fine pointed brush, paint the space where they were with a very dilute wash of raw umber and white to suggest a light-colored grout.

PAINTS	EQUIPMENT
Burnt sienna	Chalk line
Payne's grey	Large school
Yellow ochre	blackboard
Burnt umber	compass
White	Long piece of string
(I used fluid	Masking tape
acrylics which	Tape measure
are very strong	Pencil
pigments in	Compass
dilute form)	Square-edged sponge
	(e.g. a car-washing
	sponge or similar),
	cut into pieces

The Arch

My first request when planning this trompe l'oeil was that the entire room be repainted using a color which although might appear white to the casual onlooker, was most definitely not (0705Y10R, which is a sort of creamy, greeny, pale grey). Trompe l'oeil cannot work on a white surface as there is no room for highlights to stand out. (Look at the difference between the color outside the arch and the color inside.)

The idea was to make the arch look as though it had been built with the same kind of stone used in the construction of the fireplace on the facing wall. This meant that I had something to refer to for color guidance and texture.

An arch is the top half of an oval or ellipse. Steps 1 and 2 show how to draw an ellipse – for the arch you will only need the upper half.

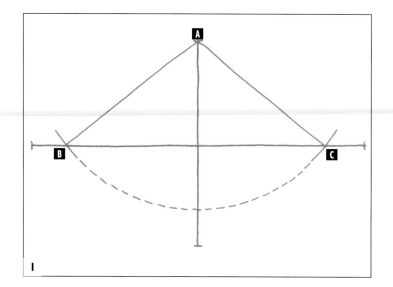

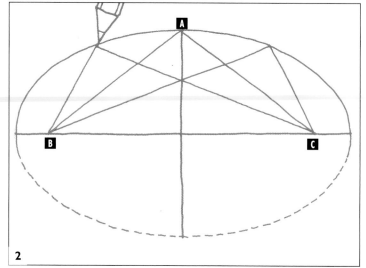

1 To draw the shape of the larger arch, first 'ping' a straight horizontal line with the chalk-line starting from the point where the curve of the arch begins on one side (at the 'front' of the arch) and meeting the same point on the other side. Make sure the starting points are level. This line forms the major axis (or width) of the ellipse. At right angles to the major axis and in the middle, you can draw the minor axis. Half of this is the distance from the major axis to the full height of the arch. You only use the top portion for the arch.

Using the blackboard compass, open the compass to half the length of the major axis (i.e. from the middle to one end). Hold the compass steady and put the point of the compass on the top of the minor axis (point A), and mark where the pencil in the compass crosses each side of the major axis. These form points B and C.

2 Next, cut a piece of string long enough to be anchored at points B and C and to be pulled up in the middle to reach point A. Using masking tape, firmly attach the ends of the string to points B and C. Using your finger at first, tuck your finger inside the loop of string and pull your finger round in an arc – you will see that your finger makes an ellipse which begins at the end of the major axis (i.e. the side of the arch) and meets the top of the minor axis (top of the arch). Now change the finger for a pencil, and do the same. Note that when you do the back edge of the arch (i.e. the same arch in perspective), you do exactly the same, taking the height of the top (minor axis) as if the arch were squared off as shown in the diagram on page 123. The starting points for the curve in perspective where the major axis sits will be found by going to the vanishing point from the same place in the full-size arch, crossing the vertical back edge of the opening.

3 To draw the outer arch shapes which you need for painting the stone architrave, you need an ordinary compass and a pencil. Follow the first arch shape as drawn above exactly with the needle of the compass, thus allowing the pencil to draw a replica where you want it. Adjust the compass width and repeat this several times to make the other shapes of the architrave.

4 Now you are ready to paint. All the work in this mural on the stonework was done with an ordinary square sponge, cut into fragments with one straight edge, which helped to follow the drawn guidelines. The sponge gives a gritty look to the painting. I used fluid acrylics here but I could easily have used diluted heavy body acrylics in thin washes. The colors were mixtures of burnt sienna, Payne's grey, yellow ochre, burnt umber and white.

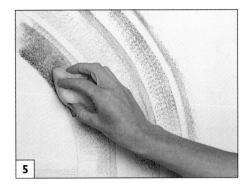

5 Build up the effect in layers, always keeping the profile of the architrave fixed in your mind, in order to be aware of the shadows and highlights.

6 White mixed with a little of the other colors is used to highlight the curves which face the light, burnt umber and Payne's grey in the shadows.

7 Keep overpainting the stonework with the same colors until the texture really gives you the feeling of stone.

PAINTS

Full palette of
  colors (see
  page 51)

EQUIPMENT

Fine pointed sable
  or nylon brush
Straight-edge
  (I use a piece of
  timber, rounded
  on one side, with
  a simple handle
  stuck to it – see
  page 43)
Long piece of
  string
8 mm (⅜ in) flat
  brush

The Books

The books were a light-hearted trompe l'oeil exercise, with a touch of humor in the imaginary titles on the spines! Some of the titles of the books were a little far-fetched, but I had a lot of fun doing them.

The books are located in the imaginary library upon fictitious shelves. Because their top and bottom edges are parallel to the direction of the viewer's feet (see page 30), these edges can be drawn using the central vanishing point on the eye-level. I attached a long piece of string to this vanishing point with masking tape (only use tape if the surface is very stable, which it should be if everything has been prepared properly, otherwise try adhesive putty), so that I could pull it out to meet the corners of the spines and easily draw the sides of the books in the correct perspective.

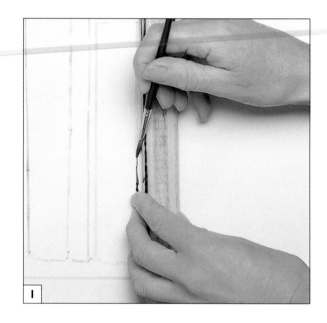

1 Start by drawing in the spines of the books in the correct position using very dilute color, a fine pointed brush and the straight edge. It's easy to wipe the paint off if you are not happy with what you've drawn, as long as you do it immediately. Do look at a real bookshelf, preferably with the same sort of books on it. Notice how the edges that recede away from you follow a route towards the central vanishing point (see page 20). The spines of the books are simple shapes – like long rectangles.

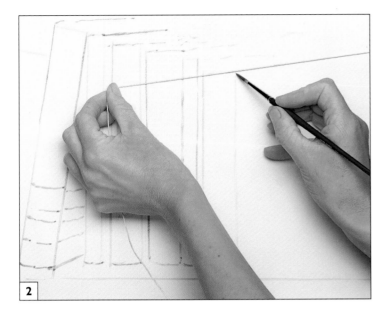

2 Attach a long piece of string to the central vanishing point (see page 20) and stretch it over to meet the tops of the spines. This helps to draw the edges which are parallel to the direction of view (in other words are parallel to the direction of your feet as you face the painting). These edges form the tops and bottoms of the sides of the books.

3 Using the straight edge as a rest for your brush (not as a masking device), start blocking in the spines and sides roughly, being as inventive as you can with colors. (You can make a straight edge with an old ruler and a couple of blobs of masking tape or adhesive putty just to keep the edge off the surface).

4 Keep the light source firmly in your mind, describing little shadows in between leaning books which you can spot by observation. This will begin to build depth into the painting.

5 Always make the visible tops (those below the eye-level) go towards the vanishing point. Gradually increase the detail, resorting often to observation for ideas. There is no finite version of this particular exercise. It's finished when you've had enough, but the more patience you can muster, the better the end result! By continuing to paint light and shade and all the little details on the covers you can achieve a really three-dimensional shelf of books. Then you can have fun with the lettering!

The Urn and Carrots

This urn forms part of the design I made for the same room in which I painted the Arches. Centrally positioned on the facing wall to the main mural is a beautiful French stone fireplace, from which I copied the 'stonework' throughout the project. To the left of this fireplace was an empty wall ideal for a smaller painting like this, whilst still keeping the same theme of the 'stone'. An urn set into an alcove is an appealing subject because it really gives you the opportunity to play with light and shade in quite a sophisticated way. I found a reference picture of this urn in a magazine and it seemed to fit the overall style of the Arches painting.

The carrots in this mural were meant as a joke – my client had a passion for carrot juice! To help me to understand the light in this painting and paint the shadows accurately, I put the carrots inside a cardboard box on its side, arranging them so that they slightly stuck out. This simulated the light conditions which would exist if the carrots were sitting in the imagined alcove.

Fruit and vegetables are very accessible to us, so when you want to paint them, first go shopping for your subject! It might help to make drawings before you start to paint and then treat the subject as a still life.

PAINTS

Payne's grey
White
Raw umber
Yellow ochre
Acrylic retarding
   medium

EQUIPMENT

Fine pointed brush
Natural sponge
   (or dishcloth)
8 mm (⅜ in) flat
   brush

The Urn

1 Start with a carefully drawn outline, paying particular attention to the way in which your eye-level might affect any round shapes involved in the painting. By this I mean that looking down on circular shapes affects them. Notice where your eye-level is in order to achieve a convincing result. At your eye-level the circle (say the top of the urn) appears as a straight line. Try observing a plate or a saucer from different angles. I sketched the outline using a thin wash of Payne's grey and white and a fine pointed brush.

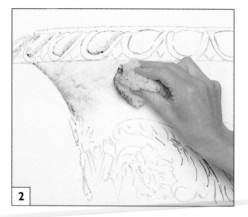

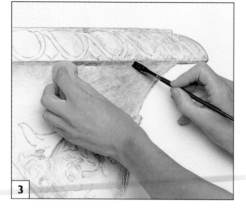

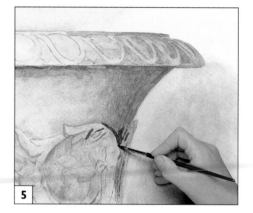

2 Build up the shadowy areas of the urn with a natural sponge using a mixture of Payne's grey, raw umber and yellow ochre. Keep the light source in your mind.

3 Continue to build light and shade using the same colors. I used a 8 mm (⅜ in) flat brush and a small natural sponge to soften the brush strokes and make the texture more exciting.

5 Carry on building depth and definition into the painting by making stronger shadows, particularly around the detailed bits, painting first with the brush then softening with the sponge.

4 Work on the background equally to show that the urn is casting a shadow on the wall of the alcove. Careful observation is the best way to understand how this works (see page 31). Try to find pictures of things in alcoves (usually statues). I used Payne's grey, yellow ochre and white to start this shadow.

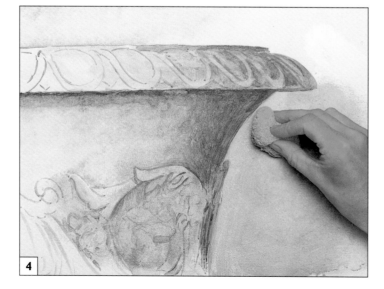

6 An acrylic retarding medium might help here to slow the drying time in order to make the edges of the shadows softer. (This is much easier to do with oil paint.) Using a small damp sponge or dishcloth helps enormously.

The Carrots

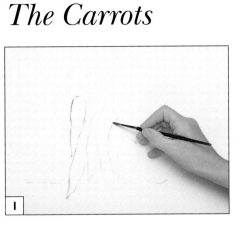

1 First, lightly sketch the outline of the bunch of carrots with diluted Payne's grey and white, using a fine pointed brush.

2 Using a full palette of colors and a 5 mm (¼ in) flat brush, start to paint directly from observation taking care to match the colors. The greens are a mixture of Jenkins green, white, yellow ochre and cadmium yellow. The carrots are built up with mixtures of cadmium red, cadmium orange, cadmium yellow, dioxazine purple and white.

3 Continue to build depth, carefully observing all the details which help to create realism, i.e. the shadows cast by the vegetables on the surfaces around them, the roundness of each shape and the feathery fronds.

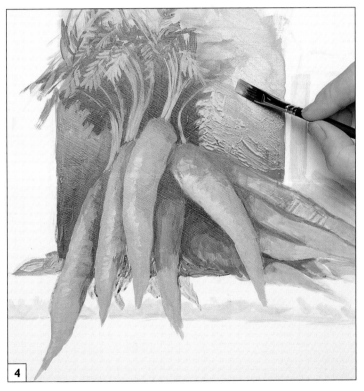

4 Keep the background abreast of the development of the vegetables – it helps to locate them in the painting. Use the flat brush for painting in the background.

5 Using a pointed brush, put deep shadows into the spaces between the carrots to make them really sit on the shelf.

PAINTS

Full palette of
  colors (see
  page 51)

EQUIPMENT

8 mm (⅜ in) flat
  brush
1 cm (½ in) flat
  brush
Fine pointed brush

Convex Mirror

On the right of the fireplace which
faces the main mural is another space
which lent itself nicely to an addition
to the whole fantasy! I thought one
might perhaps go through into
another room opposite the 'library' so
I added this painting to the original
concept for the whole room. Again, I
used the stone architrave to 'enclose'
the space. I implied a light source as
before, and continued the floor in
exactly the same way. A focal point to
which one's eye is drawn is the convex
mirror, the idea for which I borrowed
from a fifteenth-century painting by
Van Eyck called *The Arnolfini Marriage*.
In the Van Eyck painting, the backs of
the betrothed couple are reflected
and also another mysterious character.
Mine doesn't reflect anyone, but
reflects instead an imaginary room,
including a fireplace just like the real
one in the room 'next door'.

1 Start blocking in the distorted reflection with a 8 mm (⅜ in) brush. It doesn't matter how you do this – no-one will be able to tell whether it is correct or not! Just make all the straight edges bend.

3 Carry on building up detail in the reflection – the more, the merrier! I used a full palette of colors and a 8 mm (⅜ in) flat brush to do this.

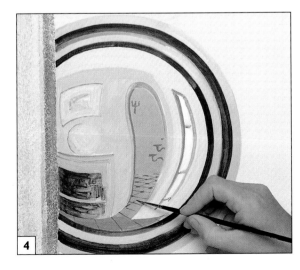

4 The floor is important and requires careful thought to make it look like a distorted version of the real floor. Add detail with the fine pointed brush.

2 The gilt frame was painted using a 1 cm (½ in) flat brush and a mix of yellow ochre, white, Jenkins green, burnt umber and Payne's grey. When you are painting something to look gold, use a lot of deep muddy greens from which brighter, paler golden-colored highlights can glow.

5 Take the fine pointed brush and add some subtle highlights to various parts of the mirror frame using white mixed with a little cadmium yellow to make the frame gleam.

Working to Commission

After painting several murals for yourself and your own home, you may find yourself being asked if you accept commissions from other people.

Assembling a portfolio

It's a good idea to assemble a portfolio of your work as soon as possible. Make it impressive by buying a good folder or portfolio, and taking great care to mount photographs graphically and neatly. Get some help doing this if you don't feel confident.

The way you photograph your work is extremely important. A decent camera is an invaluable tool for painting anyway, and a working knowledge of simple lighting will help not only with your painting but also in producing a good record for the folio. Avoid using a flash straight at the painting as it will 'burn out' the middle. Bounced light is much better, using the ceiling or a large white reflector, which could be another wall in the room.

Without a flash, use a fast film (400 ASA) and remember that it is difficult to hand-hold a camera when using a shutter speed less than $\frac{1}{60}$th of a second without the picture being out of focus. If you haven't got enough light, try to borrow a tripod and a cable release for the camera to minimize disturbance. Best of all, persuade an experienced friend to take the pictures for you!

Cheap film can also be a hazard. Choose a recommended brand and make sure that the film is not out of date as both these factors will affect the color quality.

Once you have started your own portfolio, keep it up to date and avoid loose photos falling out of the back of the sleeve, which is the sort of thing that detracts from your professional appearance!

Accepting a commission

If you are working for someone else and trying to arrive at a suitable fee for the job, take your time and think carefully before committing yourself. Find out from your client, if you can, how much he or she really wishes to spend before designing something that will take you a long time to paint. Your time is the main cost of the project, plus the material costs and any travelling or accommodation expenses. Your time can only be valued by you, on an hourly or daily basis. You should include in this time taken for during the preliminary design work. Having established roughly how much money is available for the work, consider how much detail you can achieve in the time paid for by that sum, making sure you also discuss at the outset who will be responsible for the other costs.

Painting takes much, much longer than other people realize, probably longer than one realizes oneself, so always err on the side of caution and add an amount that will take this into consideration. If the client takes a dim view of the cost, suggest a simpler design, rather than agreeing to do the job more cheaply. Every muralist can easily be replaced with another. You will be judged upon the basis of work that you have previously completed, your professionalism during meetings and discussions about the mural, and upon the presentation of ideas and drawings as quickly as possible after the first meeting.

At the outset, before the deal has been struck, do sketches for free (unless your reputation is of sufficiently high standing that this is not necessary). Once an idea has been agreed upon, the subject of money can be discussed and you can break the job into two parts. Firstly, the design, and secondly, the execution of the mural. You must be paid for doing a proper color design which constitutes the basis for the painting, and this should form the first part of the commission itself and should be adhered to during the project, so that you know exactly what you are expected to do, and the client knows exactly what to expect. Ask for an advance payment once the commission is definite, and a letter of confirmation, agreeing price based on your design and any time constraints involved. Ask for either one third of the whole price or one half. Do not start work until all is settled. If you received a third in advance, then get another third once things are visibly well under way, with the balance to be paid upon completion. All this should be set out in a proper invoice. Payment upon completion means just that. It means that you have really finished the job and seen to its varnishing, hanging of panels and so on.

Other advice I can offer which might help the budding muralist on the road to success is the same sort of advice one would give to any prospective job hunter:

• Be on time for meetings.

• Be endlessly patient and helpful with suggestions and ideas for the design.

• Get your ideas down to scale on paper in a neat and well thought-out way as soon as possible, preferably in color, and always try to give your client credit for their own ideas – even if you end up doing something completely different, they will like you for it.

• Once you have agreed terms, order the paints and start the job. Get on with it every day and try not to become distracted by other commitments which may slow you down. Once someone has decided to have a mural, they want it finished straight away. Nothing is worse than looking at a half-painted wall.

• Be pleasant to have around, so that your presence will be missed later. This adds to your chances of securing the next commission.

• Take great care not to drop paint on the floor, or leave marks in the sink, and never, ever leave painted footprints anywhere in the building. Always tidy away your paints and tools at the end of each day.

Painting Dimensions

If you wish to reproduce any of the murals shown in this book, you can of course do so at any size. However, here are the actual sizes I painted them:

Tuscan View, page 62: 2.5 m (8 ft) high x 1.5 m (5 ft) wide

Tabby Cat, page 70: life-size

Guinea Fowl, page 74: life-size

Cows Murals, page 78: 1.5 m sq (5 ft sq)

En Grisaille, page 82: life-size

Changing Room, page 88: 2.8 m (9 ft) high x 5 m (16 ft) wide

The Monk, page 94: 2.8 m (9 ft) high x 1.5 m (5 ft) wide, figure is life-size

A Cornish Window, page 98: 1 m (3 ft) high x 1.2 m (4 ft) wide

The White Horses, page 104: main wall 2.8 m (9 ft) high x 11 m (36 ft) wide, side wall 2.8 m (9 ft) high x 6 m (20 ft) wide

Painted Furniture, page 114: approx 1 m (3 ft) high x 0.6 m (2 ft) wide

Tiepolo Mural, page 118: 2.5 m (8 ft) high x 1.4 m (4½ ft) wide

The Arches, page 120: 2.5 m (8 ft) high x 2.5 m (8 ft) wide, urn 1.5 m (5 ft) high x 1 m (3 ft) wide, smaller arch 2.5 m (8 ft) high x 1.2 m (4 ft) wide

Addresses

UNITED STATES AND CANADA

The paints and supplies mentioned in this book should be available at your local home improvement or craft store. Check your Yellow Pages for the location nearest you or contact any of the suppliers listed below.

Back Street, Inc.
3905 Steve Reynolds Blvd.
Norcross, GA 30093
Tel: (770) 381-7373
Fax: (770) 381-6424

CraftCo Industries, Inc.
410 Wentworth Street North
Hamilton, Ontario
Canada L8L 5W3
Web site: http://www.craftco.com

Delta Technical Coatings
2550 Pellissier Place
Whittier, CA 90601
Tel: (800) 423-4135
Web site: http://www.deltacrafts.com

Hobby Lobby
7707 SW 44th Street
Oklahoma City, OK 73179
Tel: (405) 745-1100
Web site: http://www.hobbylobby.com

Home Depot U.S.A., Inc.
2455 Paces Ferry Road
Atlanta, GA 30339-4024
Tel: (770) 433-8211
Web site: http://www.homedepot.com

Michael's Arts & Crafts
8000 Bent Branch Drive
Irving, TX 75063
Tel: (214) 409-1300
Web site: http://www.michaels.com

Pearl Paint
308 Canal Street
New York, NY 10013
Tel: (212) 431-7931
Web site: http://www.pearlpaint.com

Silver Brush Limited
92 Main Street, Bldg. 18C
Windsor, NJ 08561
Tel: (609) 443-4900
Fax: (609) 443-4888

This book is dedicated to Derek, without whose support I could not have done it, let alone worked out how to turn the computer on… or off, for that matter!

First published in North America
in 2000 by North Light Books
an imprint of F&W Publications, Inc.
1507 Dana Avenue
Cincinnati, OH 45207

First published in 2000 by
New Holland Publishers (UK) Ltd
London • Cape Town • Sydney • Auckland

10 9 8 7 6 5 4 3 2 1

ISBN 1 58180 097 5

Project Editor: Gillian Haslam
Assistant Editor: Kate Latham
Photographer: John Freeman
Designer: Roger Daniels

Editorial Direction: Yvonne McFarlane

Reproduction by Modern Age Repro House Ltd, Hong Kong
Printed and bound in Singapore by Tien Wah Press (Pte) Ltd

Acknowledgments

I started running courses at our farm in Cornwall after an article in a magazine published a picture of a mural and mentioned that I would give tuition. During the last few years it has giving me enormous pleasure to pass on what I've learnt myself from my teachers: Ken Hill, my father, mother and in particular my sister Gillian whose genius for perspective has been an absolute inspiration.

My friend Robert Peacop at The Paint Centre in West Drayton in Middlesex has endlessly given me advice regarding materials on request and without hesitation, and for that I am also extremely grateful as the advice he has given has been sound and reliable during difficult projects.

In the recent couple of years I am also lucky to have been supported by Jason Mackie at the John Jones Art Centre in London. He has promptly supplied materials of outstanding quality, both for the presentation of this book and for paintings that I have undertaken professionally and to work with such excellent paints as the Golden range of acrylics has kick-started every painting giving me the confidence to attempt almost anything!

The Consortium for Purchasing and Distribution kindly loaned the blackboard compass featured on page 43. The unpainted firescreen on page 114 was kindly given by Scumblegoosie and the architect's rules were kindly loaned by the London Graphic Centre.

I'd like to thank people for whom I have painted murals for allowing them to be photographed during the writing of this book. Very special thanks to the Nare Hotel, Carne Beach, Veryan, Truro TR2 5PF Tel: 01872 501 111, Mr and Mrs Oliver Joanes, the Watergate Bay Hotel, Watergate Bay, Nr Newquay, Cornwall TR9 4AA, Tel: 01637 860 543, Mr and Mrs Derek Jarrett, Paul and Jo Stretton-Downes, and David Bennett. Also a big thank you to Judy Lobb who helped in the nick of time to get it all finished.

Last but not least I'm indebted to Yvonne McFarlane who has given me the chance to do this book (and the computer to do it on), and to Gillian Haslam, John Freeman and Roger Daniels who helped me to understand how to!

Index

Figures in *italics* refer to figure and illustration captions

A

acetates, overhead projector 44
  pens for 44, *44*, 46
acrylic paints *33*, 38, 39
  diluting 40
  as primers 36
  storing 47, *47*, 54
  varnishing *33*, 40
acrylic sealers 35, 36
acrylic varnish *33*, 40
aerial perspective 45, 54
air compressors 45
angles:
  assessing *19*, 22
  measuring with protractor 22, 26, 28
animals and birds:
  dog 62, 68, *68*
  Guinea Fowl *57*, 74-77
  horses 108, *108*
  Pegasus 86, *86-87*
  Tabby Cat 70-73
Arches, The *20*, *23*, *24*, 120-137
architects' drafting film, painting on 38
architectural features:
  arches *10*, 121, 128, *128-129*
  balustrades 66, *66-67*, *85*
  columns *29*, *53*, 106, *106-107*
  and lighting 15
  and use of projector 58
  see also buildings

B

background color 50
  painting colorwash 55-56
balustrades 66, *66-67*, *85*
bird's-eye views see plans
blocking in color *59*, 59-60
books on shelves 30, 130, *130-131*
boxes, storage 42
browns, mixing *53*
brushes 33, 41, *41*
  alternatives to 41-42
  for priming 38

washing 41
buildings *20*, *21*, 22, 24, *29*, *30*
  pitched roofs *21*

C

canvas, painting on 38
carrots 133, *135*
Cat, Tabby 70-73
Cattle Murals *40*, 78-81
cement render, working on 34
chalk lines 42, *43*, 58
Changing Room 89-93
clothes *91*, *96*, *96-97*
clouds 112, *113*
colors 50
  background 50, 55-56
  blocking in *59*, 59-60
  matching to color index 50-51, *55*
  mixing 52, *53*, 54
columns *29*, *53*, 106, *106-107*
compasses 43, 43-44, *44*
containers, paint 47, *47*
Convex Mirror 136, *137*
copying designs 15
  see also tracing paper, using
Cornish Window, A *13*, *24*, *25*, *26*, *26-27*, 98-103

D

details, putting in 60, 61
dishcloths 41, 46, *46*
  using 56, 59, *108*, 109, *113*, *119*
dogs 62, 68, *68*
doors, drawing 28
  see also Tuscan View
dottles 45
driers, liquid 40, *40*

E

elevations *23*
emulsion paint 50
  as primer 36
En Grisaille 82-87
enlarging drawings 15

squaring up *57*, 57-58
  see also scale drawings
equipment 42-47
  see also brushes; paints
erasers, putty 44, 46
'eyeballing' 22, 23
eye-level, positioning 16, *18*, 22, 24

F

fabric effects *90*, 116, *117*
  see also clothes
fire regulations 40
fireplace, 'marble' and 'mosaic' 8
Firescreen, The 114-117
floor protection 49
floorcloths 41, 46
  see dishcloths
floors:
  stone 64, *64-65*
  tiled *30*, 121, 126, *126-127*
flowers *13*, 100, 102, *102-103*
foxglove pink, mixing *53*
furniture, painting 115

G

gesso primer, acrylic 36
  applying to MDF panels 38
glazing 96, 97, 126
glazing mediums 39
greens, mixing *53*
Guinea Fowl *57*, 74-77

H

horses:
  heads 108, *108*, see White Horses, The
  Pegasus 86, *86-87*
human anatomy *90*

I

ideas, gathering *14*, 14-15

L

ladders 42
layout paper 47
light and shade 15, *31*, 60-61, *61*
lighting murals 15
limewashed walls 35-36

M

magazines: as ideas sources 14, *14*, 15
mail order catalogues 39
masking tape *43*, 46-47
MDF (medium density fibreboard) panels 37-38
  priming 38
  see also panels
Mirror, Convex 136, *137*
Monk, The 37, 94-97
monochromatic effects
  see En Grisaille
'mosaic' panels 8
mythological figures *85*, *86-87*

N

Nare Hotel, Cornwall 89

O

oil paints 40
  drying 40, *40*
  primers 36
  removing 36
  safety precautions 38-39
one-point perspective 24, *25*
overhead projectors
  see projectors

P

paints 33
  see acrylic paints; colors; emulsion paint; oil paints; primers
palette knives *41*, 47
palettes 47

panels 33, 36-37
  fixing 37
  MDF (medium density
    fibreboard) 37-38
  priming (MDF) 38
  transporting 37
  see Monk, The; Tuscan View
paper, layout 47
parallel rules 44
Pegasus 86, *86-87*
perspective 16
  aerial 45, 54
  establishing main viewpoint 16,
    17
  and eye-level 16, 18
  and picture plane *19*
  problems *29*
  one-point 24, *25*
  and spacing *30*
  three-point *21*, 24, *25*
  two-point 24, *25*
  and vanishing points *20, 21*, 22
photographic references 15, 49,
  68, 70
picture planes 15, *19*
  tipping 94
pink, mixing *53*
plans (bird's-eye views) *23, 25,
  26-27*
plaster walls 34
  drying time 34
  priming 36
plumb-lines 42
  using 58
primers/priming:
  MDF panels 38
  walls 36
projection method, using 26,
  26-27, 28
projectors, overhead 44
  using *49, 58-59, 59*
protractors *44*, 46
  using 22, 26, 28
putty rubbers (erasers) *44*, 46

R

radiator rollers 42, *42*
  using *93, 107*
rag-rolling 56
rags 46
reducing drawings 15
  see *also* scale drawings
reflections, painting:
  Convex Mirror 136, *137*
  water *31, 111*
repetitive shapes 66
retarders 39, *134*
rollers, paint 41-42, *42*
  using 56, 86
  see *also* radiator rollers
roofs, pitched *21*
rubbers, putty *44*, 46
rule(r)s:
  parallel *44*
  scale 23, 44, *44*, 46
  steel 44, *44*
  straight edges 43, *43*

S

sable brushes *41*
safety precautions 36, 38-39
sandpaper, using:
  to remove old paint 36
  for texture 56, 60, *65*
scaffolding 42
scale drawings, making 23-24, 44,
  46
scale rulers 23, 44, *44*, 46
sea 102, 109, *110-111*
sealants 35, 36
set squares 44
shadows *31, 61, 68, 134, 135*
shields, stainless steel 43, *43*
sketching with paint 56, 58
skies:
  blocking in 59, *59-60*
  mixing colors for *51, 52, 52,
    54-55*
  painting *112, 113*

spacing in perspective *30*
sponges 41, 46, *46*
  using 46, *86, 93, 107, 129*
spray equipment 45
squaring up designs 57, *57-58*
squirrel brushes 41
stencils 47, 66, *66-67*, 80
stepladders 42
stone floors 64, *64-65*
stonework 92, *93*
  see *also* columns
straight edges 43, *43*
stripping paint 35-36
swimming pools 40
  priming walls 36
  see White Horses, The
sword-line brushes 41, *41, 103*

T

Tabby Cat 70-73
texture:
  creating with sandpaper 56, 60,
    65
  creating with sponges 46, *93,
    107*
  from rough wall surface *35, 85*
three-point perspective *20*, 24, *25*
Tiepolo Mural 35, *118-119*
tiled floors *30, 121, 126, 126-127*
toothbrushes 41, 46
  paint flicking 40, 56, *65, 69, 86,
    87, 93, 119*
tower scaffolding 42
tracing paper, using 14-15, 24, 47,
  76, 117
transferring designs to walls
  57-59
trees, painting *53*, 80, *81*
triangles, right-angled 42, *43*
Tuscan View 6, 16, *17, 18*, 24,
  62-69
two-point perspective 24, *25*

U

underwater, paints for 40
Urn and Carrots *61, 132-135*

V

vanishing points:
  central *20*, 22
  finding 22
  other *21, 22*
varnishing acrylic paints *33*, 40
vertical lines, drawing:
  with chalk line 42
  in perspective *21, 24, 30*
video cameras, using 15
viewpoint, establishing main 16,
  17
village, Tuscan 69, *69*

W

walls:
  cement rendered 34
  plastered 34
  priming 36
  rough and uneven *35, 85*
  sealing 35
  stripping paint from 35-36
  white *91, 128*
washes, background 55-56
water reflections *31, 111*
Watergate Bay Hotel, Cornwall
  see White Horses, The
white 52
  shades 50, *53*
White Horses, The *33, 39, 104-13*
  columns *29*, 106, *106-107*
  horses' heads 108, *108*
  sea and waves 109, *110-111*
  sky and clouds 112, *113*
white walls, painting on *91, 128*
windows:
  open see Cornish Window, A
  white frames 50, *53*
  see *also* Tuscan View
working to commission 138